To
Experience
His Presence

Paula Abbott

For copies of this book or
to book Paula Abbot for your event or church, please contact:
Paula Abbott
P.O. Box 515
Terrell, TX 75160
469-595-6630
paula@roundpenministries.org

ISBN 978-1-937862-21-3

Printed in the United States of America by Snowfall Press.

* Photographs by Hannah Hogner, Amazing Grace Photos.

This book was published by BookCrafters,
Joe and Jan McDaniel SAN-859-6352
http://bookcrafters.net
http://self-publish-your-book.com
bookcrafters@comcast.net

Foreword

After writing my first book "Choices," I felt that I needed to write another book that told my story about my life after I received Jesus Christ as my personal Lord and Savior. I had many people come to me and ask me about my relationship with Jesus. They could actually see the passion coming from my heart when I spoke about Him and my transformation. You see, I came from a place of abuse, pain and hurt to a place of love, peace and contentment.

I wrote this book to explain my journey in finding my call from God. I wanted to write a book that helped others understand the love that Jesus has for each of us and how we can Experience His Presence. This book will take you through the journey that I took after I received Jesus as my Lord and Savior. Before I received my Salvation through the Blood of Jesus Christ I was an abused woman full of pain and hurt. I had been abused for 36 years from many different people and I needed to learn how to receive the forgiveness and the love of Jesus and through time I did. I share in this book my journey through trusting God and how I became a woman that truly understood the peace and love that Jesus offered through His Blood at Salvation. It took lots of hard work, but I did it with the help of the Holy Spirit. This was something I wanted so badly, and I knew that I had to make a decision to follow it all the way through. It took commitment and determination on my part, but that was something that I was willing to do. I needed a change in my life and I knew that it would take lots of work from God and from me.

In this book I will take you through the amazing journey that I took to become deeper in love with God; to find that place of peace and love that He offers. I will teach you how to walk with Him, how to talk to Him and to trust Him with your life. I'll show you how to rebuild your life one stone at a time and how to let go of the past and grab hold of the future that lies before you. There is so much joy on this side of life and I can help you find it through the love of Jesus Christ.

So come along and experience the peace and love of being in the presence of our Lord and Savior. Once you experience this place you'll never let go.

About the Author

Paula Abbott was born and raised in West Texas. She is a Texas girl through and through. Being around cattle and horses her whole life placed a love for the western culture deep down inside her soul. In 1999, Paula met and married a cowboy from Amarillo, Texas, Toby Abbott. Paula is a mother of three grown children, two teenage step children and two beautiful granddaughters.

Paula Abbott is the Co -Pastor of a Cowboy Church just east of Dallas, Texas. She is an Evangelist and an Inspirational Speaker to people of all walks of life. She travels throughout the United States bringing a message of hope to the hurting. She has connected with many people concerning everyday life and the difficult subjects that we all face day to day. In her messages she shares about her life journeys and you will witness a powerful testimony about how God turned her life as a victim into a true story of victory. Paula is passionate about teaching the true Word of God and how the Holy Spirit is here to empower each of us, so that we can walk in the fullness of God's call.

Table of Contents

Foreword

About the Author

Chapter 1
In His Presence

Proverbs 8:17
I love all who love me.
Those who search will surely find me.

Have you ever said, "Lord if only I could stay in Your Presence, things would be so amazing?" This has been my prayer for years. Every day I have prayed "Lord how can I stay right here, how can I stay and bask in Your Presence? I don't want to ever leave." I have never wanted to leave that safe and secure place of being in the Presence of God. Staying in His Presence is the place most people long to be. It's a place of safety, peace, comfort, stillness and love. In the verse above, Proverbs 8:17 tell us "those who search will surely find me." God is not far away, He is right there waiting for you to reach out to Him, to experience His Presence and His peace. Life can be so stressful and so overwhelming, we are all looking for that place where we can feel loved and feel peace. So come along with me as I share my journey and invite you to enter into His Presence.

After I received Jesus Christ as my Lord and Savior in 1997, I had to learn to find and keep His peace in my life. I was saved and I had my name written in the Lambs' book of Life, which means I will spend eternity with Jesus. This in itself was the most amazing thing I have ever done, but it wasn't enough, I wanted more. I wanted more of Jesus in my life. I wanted to experience His Presence and I wanted to stay there.

Day after day I would struggle to find peace in my life, and struggled I did for many years, even after receiving Christ as my Lord and Savior. The reason that I struggled is because I didn't know how to experience His Presence. I didn't know how to search for Him and His peace. After 36 years of physical, mental, emotional and verbal abuse, I was full of rejection and pain. I didn't know there actually could be anything good or peaceful come from my life. I have met so many people that have accepted the Lord as their personal savior, but still had a longing in their hearts they didn't understand. A longing for more of God, or a longing for peace in their hearts, or maybe a longing for unconditional love. If this is your situation, I am so glad that you are reading this book, because I know that you will be able to experience the contentment, the joy, and the peace that I did when I experience His Presence.

As soon as I received Christ as the Lord of my life, I had to step out in faith and learn to find that peace only He could bring into my life. My spirit was born again; I had been made a new person in Christ Jesus as 2 Corinthians 5:17 tells us - *Therefore, if anyone is in Christ, he is a new creation; old things have passed away; behold, all things have become new.* I really knew this to be true, but I still had a flesh that I had to contend with. I knew that my spirit was born again full of Jesus Christ, but I still had an old worldly flesh. I wanted the peace of God, I wanted to be in the Presence of God, but my flesh wanted to stay in the world. It was as if I had a war going on inside of me. One tugging this way and one tugging that way, I felt torn between what I wanted in my spirit and what I wanted in my flesh.

I wanted to continue doing the things that I had always done, but something inside my spirit was crying out for something different, something new and peaceful. I struggled day and night looking for the answers. I didn't have a Bible, more over I didn't even know how to read and understand the Bible. You see my adopted father was an atheist and we never talked about God or His son Jesus. We never went to Church or talked of His love for us. So I was brand new in this Jesus thing, but I knew that I wanted it with everything inside me and that's when God sent me an angel in human form. My husband, Toby Abbott, is a real man in love with God. He knew the Word of God and had been a Christian for most of his life. He knew what I needed and the best thing he had to offer me was patience. He was very patient in teaching me and leading me. I guess I can say the best way Toby taught me the Word of God was by him living it out loud for me to see. His everyday life was a sermon that spoke straight to me. He lived his life as a man of God and lived each day as an example for me to follow and he still does today.

I received my first Bible in the year 2000 and it was like God had opened the doors to the flood gates in my heart. I was so thirsty for this place of peace and love that I searched for myself for what God had for me personally. I found in Jeremiah 29:13 where it tells us *"And you will seek Me and find Me, when you search for Me with all your heart."* Reading this scripture I knew I had to search Him out with all my heart, and with all my strength. I had to begin rebuilding my life, one stone at a time. I found an amazing story in the book of John. About when Jesus was at the pool of Bethesda and heals a man that had been sick for 38 years. This is a story that I really could relate to, because I was 36 when I gave Jesus my life and received Him as my personal

Lord and Savior. Let's take a look at this amazing story in John chapter 5.

John 5:1-9 *After this there was a feast of the Jews, and Jesus went up to Jerusalem. ² Now there is in Jerusalem by the Sheep Gate a pool, which is called in Hebrew, Bethesda, having five porches. ³ In these lay a great multitude of sick people, blind, lame, paralyzed, waiting for the moving of the water. ⁴ For an angel went down at a certain time into the pool and stirred up the water; then whoever stepped in first, after the stirring of the water, was made well of whatever disease he had. ⁵ Now a certain man was there who had an infirmity thirty-eight years. ⁶ When Jesus saw him lying there, and knew that he already had been in that condition a long time, He said to him, "Do you want to be made well?" ⁷ The sick man answered Him, "Sir, I have no man to put me into the pool when the water is stirred up; but while I am coming, another steps down before me." ⁸ Jesus said to him, "Rise, take up your bed and walk." ⁹ And immediately the man was made well, took up his bed, and walked. And that day was the Sabbath.*

In reading this incredible story, I saw myself in this man, more than I would like to admit. The Bible tells us in this story that this man had an infirmity for 38 years. His infirmities could have been addictions, physical sickness, or even rejection like I had. It really could have been anything; the Bible just tells us that it was just an infirmity. My infirmities were many; I was a drug addict, I was broken, I suffered with pain and loneliness, I struggled with mental and emotional abuse, I had an alcohol addiction, but most of all I was approval addicted. Approval addiction is when we need the approval of others to feel worthy.

In this story this man laid there with other sick people for 38 years, waiting for a movement of the waters. When I read that I really started to laugh because we all love to share our infirmities or our sickness with others. I guess that's where we always say, misery loves company. Boy isn't that so right? We love to hang out with other people that feed us and that understand why we are in the place we are. Actually, I feel that the sick feed off of the sick. It gives us an excuse to stay in bondage.

In this story Jesus walks up to this man, why Jesus chose this one man, we will never know, but I really believe that this man was sick and tired of being sick and tired. You know, we will never change until we are at that place where we are done with the infirmities in our lives. We have to be at that place in our lives where we say "I am done, I need to change." That was so me, I'm sure it was why Jesus chose this man as well. Jesus longs to work with someone that is ready to be worked with.

In verse 6, Jesus walked up and said "Do you want to be made well?" In other words are you done lying here? Are you ready to move on and live your life the way it was planned for you to live? The Bible doesn't say that, but I can only imagine that's how it was. Are you done? Are you ready to move on and live your life to the fullest? That's what He asked me, when I finally gave my life to Him. But then in the story the man came back with an excuse. *"Sir, I have no man to put me into the pool when the water is stirred up; but while I am coming, another steps down before me."* Isn't that exactly what we do? Make excuses for why we haven't made this change in our lives. It's always someone else's fault that we are where we are. "I have no man to put me in the pool," he said to Jesus. Jesus standing there looking him in the face, he tells Him, "I have no one to help me." Please hear me when I say this, if we wait on the perfect time or for someone else to get us out of the pit we are in, it will never come. There will never be the perfect time to make this decision; the time is here and now. We are not promised tomorrow, so the time is now, don't wait on making this change in your life.

If I had been that man and really wanted my healing, I would have inched my way to the edge of the waters and I would have hung my foot in until the angel came and "Bam" I would have been first and received my healing. Excuses are what keep us where we are, so that we don't have to put out the effort to change. So sad, but very true for many people. I can't even imagine how many excuses Jesus gets from us every day. One excuse after the other. But, Jesus being Jesus, He showed compassion for this man, as He stood there looking in his eyes.

In verse 8 Jesus healed him, He said *"Rise up, take your bed and walk,"* and I love this part because Jesus made him clean up his mess after he was made whole. Before he could start his new life, he had to clean up the mess from the past life. This is the part that was so hard for me. I would have loved to have just walked away and started my new life from scratch, but that's not how it works. We are to clean up our mess that we left behind and fix the broken bridges in our lives. We need to mend the hearts of the people we have hurt and we need to mend the relationships that we have destroyed. We need to mend the past hurts in our own hearts and forgive all the above. Was it easy for me to do this? NO, but very much needed so that I could experience His Presence with my whole heart. It was needed so that I could live my life according to His plan and His purpose for me. In Jeremiah 29:11 *"For I know the thoughts that I think toward you, says the LORD, thoughts of peace and not of evil, to give you a future and a hope."* God has planned an amazing future for us, full of love, peace and hope. This is the one thing that I will fight to keep. That way I can experience His Presence.

Chapter 2
The Rebuild

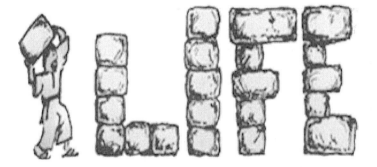

Romans 12:2
And do not be conformed to this world,
but be transformed by the renewing of your mind,
that you may prove what is good and acceptable and
the perfect will of God.

In this chapter we will be talking about the rebuilding or renewing of our souls (which is our mind, feelings and emotions). If you have received Jesus Christ as your personal Lord and Savior then your spirit has been born again, but your soul is still in the world. How can your spirit be born again? When we are born as infants we are born into a natural body made up of three (3) parts: body, soul and spirit. The body contains our five senses: taste, touch, smell, sight and hearing. Our soul is our mind, our feelings, and our emotions. Then, we have our spirit. Our spirit is created to be filled with the Spirit of God. Before we receive Jesus Christ as our personal Lord and Savior our spirit is dead. You can find this in John 3:6-7 *"That which is born of the flesh is flesh, and that which is born of the Spirit is spirit.⁷ Do not marvel that I said to you, "You must be born again."* In this passage we see that our spirit needs to be born again to receive God's Spirit which is the Holy Spirit. When we ask Jesus Christ to come into our lives and forgive us of our sins, at that very moment our spirits are born again!

After I said the prayer to receive Jesus Christ as my personal Lord and Savior, I realized that I still had my soul to deal with (that is my mind, my feelings and my emotions). This was one of the hardest things for me to understand, because I thought when I received Salvation through the blood of Jesus Christ I would just change overnight. That I would go from being a wild child right to being a saint. Well, that wasn't the case at all. After my Salvation I knew that something was different. I knew that for the first time in my life I felt complete, but I still had the same desires, thoughts and feelings that I had before I received Jesus Christ. I had thoughts and feelings that were still hanging out in the world, but deep down inside my heart I knew it was wrong. I had people telling me that it was my conscience and not the Spirit of God. I had never had a conscience before I received Jesus, so why would I have one now? When I did something wrong it never bothered me when I was a sinner. I just did it and I didn't even think twice. But after I had received Jesus as my personal Lord and Savior, I knew deep in my heart that it wasn't right having those kinds of thoughts and feelings anymore.

So here's where the rebuilding process starts. I knew it wasn't going to be easy and I had some hard work ahead of me, but I was up for the challenge. So I rolled up my sleeves and faced this challenge head on. It was kind of different for me, because I had never faced anything hard before and this would be the first time. I felt like I was being torn between two different worlds, feeling one way on the side of good and another way on the side of bad. I wanted to do what was right, but I didn't know how. All my life I had done things according to the world's ways. I had never read or heard the Word of God before my Salvation, so trying to live according to the Word of God was hard for me after my Salvation. When I first started trying to rebuild my life, I found myself falling right back into the pit of depression, pain and destruction. I would cry out to God and say "why?" His answer back to me was, "You have a choice Paula, but I'm standing right here with you, I will never leave you nor forsake you." I guess just knowing that God was there giving me the strength that I needed to get through each and every day was very comforting to my heart. Just knowing that you're not alone feels really good when you're facing a challenge. God is not in the business of overnight breakthroughs, He wants to build our faith and trust in Him. God is not going to take us away from the trials in our lives, but He will go through them with us. The Bible tells us in 1 Corinthians 10:13 *No temptation has overtaken you except such as is common to man; but God is faithful, who will not allow you to be tempted beyond what you are able, but with the temptation will also make the way of escape, that you may be able to bear it.* If God just granted everyone an overnight breakthrough then we would never learn how to stand in faith and trust Him through the storms in our lives. I knew that I didn't get into this mess overnight and knew that I wasn't getting out of it overnight either. God uses the storms in our lives to build our trust and faith in Him and to make us stronger. Not really something I wanted to go through, but something I "needed" to go through. I love it when Paul writes about the same kind of struggles in his own life.

Romans 7:14-25 *[14] So the trouble is not with the law, for it is spiritual and good. The trouble is with me, for I am all too human, a slave to sin. [15] I don't really understand myself, for I want to do what is right, but I don't do it. Instead, I do what I hate. [16] But if I know that what I am doing is wrong, this shows that I agree that the law is good. [17] So I am not the one doing wrong; it is sin living in me that does it. [18] And I know that nothing good lives in me, that is, in my sinful nature. I want* *to do what is right, but I can't. ¹⁹ I want to do what is good, but I don't. I don't want to do what is wrong, but I do it anyway. ²⁰ But if I do what I don't want to do, I am not really the one doing wrong; it is sin living in me that does it. ²¹ I have discovered this principle of life that when I want to do what is right, I inevitably do what is wrong. ²² I love God's law with all my heart. ²³ But there is another power within me that is at war with my mind. This power makes me a slave to the sin that is still within me. ²⁴ Oh, what a miserable person I am! Who will free me from this life that is dominated by sin and death? ²⁵ Thank God! The answer is in Jesus Christ our Lord.*

Doesn't this sound like the struggles we all go through every day? Well, maybe not you, but I definitely do. Looking back on the beginning of my journey with God I now see that He was right there with me through all my trials, my tears, and He was right there beside me as I stood and believed in His Word. I can see how He gave me the strength to push forward and breakthrough each and every time I came to a place in my life I needed to overcome. I know now that I am much stronger today in my faith because of this journey with God. I pray that you will find that same strength you need to overcome as well. I would like for us to go to the book of Nehemiah so that we can understand how to rebuild our lives and overcome the destruction we have caused by our wrong choices.

Let's say that you're a contractor and you've been called out on a jobsite to do a rebuild. You get to the jobsite and you see a house that has been destroyed. A good contractor would start by walking through the jobsite looking and preparing an estimate on what it would take to rebuild the structure. Then he would start by tearing down the "old" structure and completely cleaning the site so that he could rebuild a "new" structure. You see in order to have something new you need to get rid of the old. The Bible tells us in 2 Corinthians 5:17 *"Therefore, if anyone is in Christ, he is a new creation; old things have passed away; behold, all things have become new."* If you were a good contractor you would not dig a hole and push the old structure in and cover it up with dirt and then build the new structure on top. We all know when you cover something up; it will always come to the surface eventually. It never fails that when we bury things, they always make their way back to the top. Same way with our past, if we just bury them, they will come back up at the wrong time, "<u>every</u> <u>time</u>." So to have a strong and complete rebuild in our lives we need to wipe the slate clean, then we start the rebuild. Starting the demolition process is one of the hardest parts to any rebuild. Tearing down and cleaning up the mess is very labor intensive and when I say labor intensive I'm not speaking about physical labor, I'm speaking about our feelings and emotions. I found myself standing at the place of decision and like Paul in the above scripture I didn't like what I saw in myself. So when you find yourself at this stage in life, the stage of being sick and tired of being sick and tired, or maybe you're at the stage of being broke, busted and disgusted, this is a good place to start your rebuild.

If you are not willing to make a change then you will end up quitting before you ever get started. You need to have your mind set on "I will not quit, no matter how hard it gets" and I promise it does get hard, but with Jesus on your side you can do it. You can go from the place of not enough to the place of plenty. You can go from nothing positive in your life to receiving overflowing Blessings. Jesus tells us to "Rise up and walk." So today I say to you "Rise up and take back your life. Rise up and move forward in the overflowing Blessings of Jesus. Rise up my friend and start enjoying your life. Rise up my friend, rise up."

So let's start this rebuild and let's take a look at the book of Nehemiah. In chapter 1 Nehemiah starts his journey to rebuild the walls of Jerusalem that he and his people had destroyed. The walls of Jerusalem were put up to protect the people from their enemies. How many of us have destroyed the walls of protection in our lives? I can say for sure that I burnt every bridge and wall I had in my life. As we read the story of Nehemiah, I believe that God will speak to us on how to start rebuilding our lives.

Step 1 through the book of Nehemiah:

Nehemiah 1:2-4 *Hanani, one of my brothers, came to visit me with some other men who had just arrived from Judah. I asked them about the Jews who had returned there from captivity and about how things were* *going in Jerusalem. And they said to me, "The survivors who are left from the captivity in the province are there in great distress and reproach. The wall of Jerusalem is also broken down, and its gates are burned with fire." So it was, when I heard these words that I sat down and wept, and mourned for many days; I was fasting and praying before the God of heaven.*

In this passage we see that Nehemiah was told of the destruction in Jerusalem. He was told that the walls had been broken down and the gates burned with fire. Realizing what he and his people had done, Nehemiah sat down and wept and mourned for many days. This same thing happened to me when I realized what I had done in my past. It was devastating to my heart and I found myself crying out to God, "How did I get to this place in life?" I had burnt every bridge and destroyed almost every relationship in my life. I threw away everything that meant anything to me, just threw it out like left over spaghetti. I didn't even think twice, I just did it. I had hurt so many people that tried to love me. I was living a life of self-pity and selfishness, blaming everyone else for my wrong choices. I only thought of myself and what I wanted, I didn't care about anyone else or their needs. When I looked at the person I had become and realized I was living a life of sin, I had to make a decision to take that first step out of the darkness of the pit and into the sunshine. I think I actually sat down wept and mourned for many days like Nehemiah. Realizing what we have done is the first step in our journey to rebuilding our lives. So looking at this passage Nehemiah is forced to realize what had happened in Jerusalem and he had to make a decision and face his part in this destruction.

Step 2 through the book of Nehemiah:

Nehemiah 1: 5-7 And I said: "I pray, LORD God of heaven, O great and awesome God, You who keep Your covenant and mercy with those who love You and observe Your commandments, please let Your ear be attentive and Your eyes open, that You may hear the prayer of Your servant which I pray before You now, day and night, for the children of Israel Your servants, <u>***and confess the sins***</u> *of the children of Israel which we have sinned against You. Both my father's house and I have sinned. We have acted very corruptly against You.*

Here in this passage we see that Nehemiah asked God to forgive the sins of himself and his people. After we realize what we have done we need to ask God to forgive us. I'm going to ask you to read the scripture again, but slowly this time.

Did you feel the heart felt prayer from Nehemiah? This wasn't some ol' "I'm kinda sorry God" prayer; this was a true heart felt prayer, asking God to forgive him and his people. I can just see Nehemiah on his knees weeping out to God with all his heart. "Please God forgive me and my people for we have acted very corruptly against you." Being a Co-Pastor in our Church

I see many people who come to the alter crying out to God with a halfhearted prayer. Sounding something like this, "God I'm sorry that I got caught, if you'll help me out this time I promise to do better." Kinda like there you go God I'm confessing now fix it. But then I have seen people who have come down to the alter and fallen on their knees and wept straight from their hearts for the things they have done. They have cried out to God for forgiveness and I believe in my heart that they had a true heart felt confession. They are the ones who have asked God to forgive their sins not just cover them up. This is what Nehemiah did; he made a heartfelt confession to God and asked Him to forgive the sins that he and his people caused and that he was ready to rebuild what he had destroyed. Yep, I was there myself down on my knees crying out to God. "Please forgive me for everything I have done." I think my exact words were "Help me to help myself, Lord." I didn't have in me what I needed to help myself, but I knew with the Blood of Jesus I could overcome anything. That's a great place to start, on your knees with an open heart and with your ears ready to hear from God. I heard a statement from a friend of mine and it really ministered to my heart and I want to share it with you. "When you turn over a new 'leaf' it doesn't mean that you are changing who you are. You will still be the same 'tree.' It just means that you will be using a different branch to feel the sunshine of life." So remember when you are in this stage of rebuilding and changing your life you are still you, but now you'll just enjoy the sunshine of life a lot more.

Step 3 through the book of Nehemiah:

Nehemiah 2:6 The king, with the queen sitting beside him, asked, "How long will you be gone? When will you return?" After I told him how long I would be gone, the king agreed to my request.

In this passage we see that Nehemiah went to the King to ask his permission to go back and rebuild the walls in Jerusalem. The King asked "How long will it take? When will you return?" Does this phrase sound familiar to you? How long will it take you to get better? When will we see a change in you? Let me be very honest, when you make the decision to change your life, your friends and family will not understand the process that it takes. Sometimes you will feel completely alone, but Jesus said "I will never leave you nor forsake you." I heard over and over from my family and friends, "How long is it going to take? When will we see a change in you?" All these questions I couldn't answer because I didn't know how long it would take. At that point in my life I was in a deep dark pit of destruction and had a lot of work ahead of me. I didn't get there overnight and I knew that I wasn't getting out overnight either. Don't put a time limit on your rebuild; you need to take it one day at a time. I'm so very happy that God didn't ask me to correct all my faults at one time. He worked with me on one thing and then when I overcame that, we started on something new and as of today I am still working and rebuilding my life. Rebuilding your life is going to be a marathon not a sprint. Take Him by the hand and walk with Him, this is a new beginning for you, it is worth it.

Nothing is too hard for you to overcome; you can do anything that you put your whole heart to do. I remember a few years ago I started walking in the mornings for exercise and I would see people jogging and wished I could jog like they did. I had never been a person that liked to walk, much less run. So every time I tried to jog I had excuses on why I couldn't, so I just kept walking. Until one day God told me "Paula if you never try you'll never know if you can or not, so just try." That touched my heart in a big way, so I started jogging a little each day and then each day I did a little more and before I knew it I was jogging half of the course. If you'll put out the effort then God will meet you there, but if you never try you'll never know if you could have done it or not. So step out today and take the challenge in rebuilding your life, I promise it will be worth it in the long run! Take your time and make sure you don't let friends and family rush you, because when you feel rushed you will most likely give up before you reach your goal. It doesn't matter how long it takes, God has all the time in the world to work with you. Take your time and do it right the first time.

Step 4 through the book of Nehemiah:

Nehemiah 2:11-14 So I came to Jerusalem and was

there three days. Then I arose in the night, I and a few men with me; I told no one what my God had put in my heart to do at Jerusalem; nor was there any animal with me, except the one on which I rode. And I went out by night through the Valley Gate to the Serpent Well and the Refuse Gate, and viewed the walls of Jerusalem which were broken down and its gates which were burned with fire. Then I went on to the Fountain Gate and to the King's Pool, but there was no room for the animal under me to pass.

Can you say destruction? We can see from this passage that Nehemiah is standing in a place of total destruction. I can only imagine what it looked like. This would be the place that I call the "The Danger Zone." This step in our rebuild is the danger zone for many, many people. This is a place where you make the decision to run or to stay. This was a very hard place for me, because I was a person that didn't like to face myself. I was one that ran away from everything and I didn't like pressure of any kind. If it was too hard then I didn't do it. When I stood there and took a long look at my life and everyone that I had destroyed while I was in a state of selfishness, I wanted to run and fast.

I'm sure that most of you who are reading this book today have not always been saints and I did say most of you. I'm sure that we have all been to a party or two in our lives. I had lots of parties in my day and the bigger the better. It was almost an everyday event for me.

21

Now the day after, "The Clean Up" was not my favorite part at all. I can't really think of anyone who likes that part. The party would get out of control every time, but while you're in the moment drinking and hanging with friends you really don't think about the day after. This is where we find Nehemiah in this scripture, we find him standing in the middle of a disaster area and now it's time to clean up the mess. Sure sounds like the "day after" to me, doesn't it? This would have been a really great time for him to turn around and leave, but he didn't, he had made a commitment to God. I have been faced with this very same thing many times and a decision to run or stay. I'm very glad to say that I decided to stay. I rolled up my sleeves, put my gloves on and I dug in with my whole heart. I was ready for a change in my life and I knew that it wasn't going to be easy, but I was up for the challenge. I knew I wasn't alone.

The first thing I did was to make a 100% commitment to follow through and to not quit. I couldn't quit on me and I couldn't quit on my family and I sure couldn't quit on Jesus Christ. It is so very important to make this commitment and follow through with it. Too many people are sitting on the fence coming to Church and living in the world at the same time and they have never made a full commitment to follow God's Word. We find it here in 1 Kings 18:21 - *Elijah challenged the people: "How long are you going to sit on the fence? If GOD is the real God, follow him; if it's Baal, follow him. Make up your minds!"* So I say to you today, get off the fence and make up your mind to follow God. I challenge you today to get in and run the race to rebuild your life! You can't go wrong.

The second thing I did was forgive myself. This was a very hard step for me, because I had really destroyed everything in my life. I was feeling all kinds of condemnation from the enemy. I couldn't look at myself in the mirror and not see the choices that I had made. But, one day I heard the Lord say to me "Paula you can't turn back time, you can't have do overs in life, so you need to let it go and focus on the present and your future" and that was just what I needed to hear. I stepped out and I forgave myself, it took me a while, but I did it and now when I look in the mirror I see "Grace" and not sin.

The third thing I did was forgive others. I had to forgive everyone that had hurt me in my past. I had to let it go and forgive them. I truly believe that healing comes to those with a forgiving heart.

The fourth thing I did was ask for forgiveness from my family and friends. Some forgave me and some did not, but that's between God and them. I'm really ok with me and I know that God has forgiven me and that's a wonderful feeling. Forgiveness is the corner stone in your rebuild. When you have done all four of these steps in forgiveness, then you are ready to start.

In Chapter 3 of Nehemiah it talks about who rebuilt

which part of the wall. Each family had their own section of wall to rebuild. I love this part, because it tells me that I only have to focus on myself and not anyone else. Don't worry about someone else and what they need to do in their lives, just worry about your part.

In Chapter 3 Nehemiah assigns each person a section of the wall that they had helped destroy. They had to make a commitment to rebuild only what they had torn down. That was really good for me, because I didn't have to worry about my family I just had to worry about myself. So if I can give you any advice don't worry about your husband, or your mom and dad, or your friends. Just worry about you and what you need to overcome. God will work in their lives. You just need to worry about yourself. This step actually allows you to take a step back and look at what is right in front of you, not what's around you. You do what you can do and leave the rest to God and before you know it you'll see a big difference in your rebuild. They will see it in you too!

Step 5 through the book of Nehemiah:

Nehemiah 4:1-2 Sanballat was very angry when he learned that we were rebuilding the wall. He flew into a rage and mocked the Jews, 2 saying in front of his friends and the Samarian army officers, "What does this bunch of poor, feeble Jews think they're doing? Do they think they can build the wall in a single day by just offering a few sacrifices? Do they actually think they can make something of stones from a rubbish heap and charred ones at that?"

We see in this passage that as soon as Nehemiah started rebuilding the walls, people came against him. They stood there and made fun of him for trying to fix what he had destroyed. When you start rebuilding your life people will make fun of you. They will come against what you are trying to do and they will try to stop you. In this stage of my rebuild, I lost all my "so called" friends. They weren't ready to make a change in their own lives and they didn't much like what I was doing. They told me that I could never do it, that I wasn't strong enough without them. They told me that I should just stay in the pit with them and give up on trying to become something better. Have you ever heard the term "misery loves company?" That is a very true statement. This step is where I had to make that decision and take a stand in what I was trying to do. I was feeling so much better about my life and I made sure I surrounded myself with positive people and God's Word to strengthen me during my rebuild. I didn't need the negative talk and negative people in my life, because it did nothing but bring me down. To be honest with you, I really didn't have any friends back then they were just all party buddies. They were just people that got caught up in my madness and destruction. They were not there to encourage me or to be a true friend. You know, you have true friends when they stand beside you and encourage you. So stay focused and do not listen to the people in the grandstands. I had a Pastor tell me once that when you're running the race of your life, do not stop and argue with the people in the grandstands. When you're on the race track and running your race, there will always be people watching from the grandstands. They will shout out negative things to try and get you to stop, but if you stop running and go up into the stands to defend yourself, you are stepping out of the race. Stay in the race; keep focused on what's in front of you. The grandstand people will always be there, don't listen to them. Stay focused and you will win every time.

Step 6 through the book of Nehemiah:

Nehemiah 4:10-12 Then the people of Judah began to complain, "The workers are getting tired, and there is so much rubble to be moved. We will never be able to build the wall by ourselves." [11] Meanwhile, our enemies were saying, "Before they know what's happening, we will swoop down on them and kill them and end their work." [12] The Jews who lived near the enemy came and told us again and again, "They will come from all directions and attack us!"

It never fails, right in the middle of your rebuild you'll find yourself complaining and saying, "It's too hard. The other life was so much easier." Yes you would be right, because it's easier to just stay in the pit and not put out any effort to change, but you will never overcome all the unhappiness if you don't move forward. If you let down your guard you will be attacked by your enemy. In 1 Peter 5:8 the Bible tells us to, *"Stay alert! Watch out for your great enemy, the devil. He prowls around like a roaring lion, looking for someone to devour."* Satan's biggest tool is complaining. Stay strong, stay in the Word, and stay hooked up with others that can strengthen you in God's Word. Build with one hand and hold your weapon (the Word of God) in the other hand. Do not let down your guard at any time. Stay alert; know who your enemy is and what his tactics are. If you will resist him he will leave, but only for a short time, then he will return. So be ready, you have the Holy Spirit to help you in this step of your rebuild. The Holy Spirit is our helper in times of need and he will never leave you nor forsake you. In Nehemiah 4:16-17 it tells us that the people built with one hand and held their weapon in the other. *So it was, from that time on, that half of my servants worked at construction, while the other half held the spears, the shields, the bows, and wore armor; and the leaders were behind all the house of Judah. [17] Those who built on the wall, and those who carried burdens, loaded themselves so that with one hand they worked at construction, and with the other held a weapon.* Hang on to the Word of God and stay focused, you can do this. I know because I did. I put my head down and I worked right through all the junk and came out on top.

At the end of Nehemiah you will see that they finished rebuilding the walls of Jerusalem 52 days later. They didn't give up and they didn't quit. They stayed focused on what they had to do, and they did it.

Mark 4-35-41 On the same day, when evening had come, He said to them, "Let us cross over to the other side." ³⁶ Now when they had left the multitude, they took Him along in the boat as He was. And other little boats were also with Him. ³⁷ And a great windstorm arose, and the waves beat into the boat, so that it was already filling. ³⁸ But He was in the stern, asleep on a pillow. And they awoke Him and said to Him, "Teacher, do You not care that we are perishing?" ³⁹ Then He arose and rebuked the wind, and said to the sea, "Peace, be still!" And the wind ceased and there was a great calm. ⁴⁰ But He said to them, "Why are you so fearful? How is it that you have no faith?" ⁴¹ And they feared exceedingly, and said to one another, "Who can this be, that even the wind and the sea obey Him!"

There will always be storms in your life and sometimes big storms are hard to go through, but as the verse mentions above, Jesus said to the storm, "Peace, be still." I believe that He is saying this to us today. Trust in Jesus to help you through the storms of life and trust Him to help you in your rebuild. If you trust Him with all your heart, you too will experience His Presence.

Chapter 3
Footprints

Ephesians 3:16
*That He would grant you, according to the riches of
His glory, to be strengthened with might through His
Spirit in the inner man,*

I have read the poem "Footprints in the Sand" many times and every time it touched my heart deeply. Not long ago my brother and I shared some stories of the times when Jesus had carried us through some really hard times and not once did we recall it being on the beach. So I begin to pray for God to give me the words and help me to rewrite this very famous poem, through the eyes of a person that has suffered many hardships in life. I have named this poem "Footprints" and I pray that it touches your life.

Footprints

One night I had a dream. I dreamed
I was walking along the beach with the LORD.
Across the sky flashed scenes from my life.
For each scene I noticed two sets of
footprints in the sand: one belonging
to me, and the other to the LORD.
When the last scene of my life flashed before me, I
looked back and I noticed
that through the hardest times in my life I was not
walking on the beach with the Lord.
I also noticed that it happened at the hardest, lowest
and saddest times in my life. This really bothered me
so I questioned the LORD about it:

"LORD, you said that once I decided to follow you,
you'd walk with me all the way. But I have noticed
that during the hardest times in my life, we were not
walking on the beach anymore. I didn't see two sets of
footprints indicating that you were still with me. I don't
understand why, when I needed you most, you would
leave me."

The LORD replied:

"My precious child, I love you and I would never leave you. During your times of pain, trials and sufferings, when you didn't feel me walking with you on the beach anymore or see two sets of footprints in the sand, it was then that I carried you. As you can see the footprints that were in the sand at the beginning where all over as we danced and celebrated the blessings in your life. When I knew hardship and pain was approaching you, I drew you closer to me. You only thought we were dancing close, you had no idea that this trial was coming to destroy you. When you see one set of footprints it was then that I carried you. The beautiful sand that we were dancing on quickly became a pile of mangled and twisted metals, sharp and jagged objects, broken glass and demons of every kind. I knew that you could not climb this mountain that was ahead of you, so I picked you up and I carried you. You had to have felt my heartbeat as I carried you, because at that moment my heart was connected to yours and we became one. Although you had to go through this trial and feel the discomfort that it brought, I want you to know that I kept you safe and I shielded you from the intense pain. Child, I took the pain that was meant for you and carried you all the way through and when it was over I set you down, back in the sand and we begin to dance again."

Chapter 4
The Change Cycle

Philippians 3:14
I press on to reach the end of the race and
receive the heavenly prize for which God,
through Christ Jesus, is calling us.

What is change? It's to make the form, nature, content, or the future course of something different from what it is now. To transfer from one place to another. How many of you reading this book right now know without a doubt that God has asked you to do something different that will bring a huge change into your life? Most likely it's something that you cannot do on your own. It will be something so difficult and hard that it will change the course of your life forever. It normally means that we have to go against everything we have been taught our whole lives. Our minds will not understand why and we will try to reason our way out of the plans God has for us. If we don't understand the when, the how and the why, we will talk our way out of it every time. But God tells us in Isaiah 55:8 *"For My thoughts are not your thoughts, nor are your ways My ways," says the LORD.* God knows the future and the outcome better than we do. So when He requires us to do something we need to trust that He knows best. It may not feel good at the beginning, but it will get easier as you go.

A few years back the Lord really started teaching me about the process the mind goes through when we are asked to make a change in our lives. I'm sure you already know, but people really don't like change! We avoid it like it's the plague. I have seen people run the other way when faced with change. So many of us never received the blessings in our lives because we run from change. We can't get from one place to the next until we travel the road in-between.

People normally have goals in their lives that they are trying to obtain or to conquer. We humans are goal oriented and we are always looking for something to work towards, if "of course" it's not too hard. Once we reach that goal, then we start looking for the next goal. These goals can be anything like, losing weight, eating better, being a better parent, maybe a better wife or husband, it could be a big career change or just trying to follow Christ the best you can, or maybe it's going into Ministry or it can be a major overhaul in your life. Whatever your goal is, it will cause change to come in your life and this is where we find ourselves either running or pushing through to obtain the goal. So I pray that this chapter touches your life and helps you to see what our minds go through each time we are faced with a new goal or change.

Why do we come against change in our lives? Why is it so hard to follow the goals that God sets for us? I feel that this chapter "The Change Cycle" will help us answer these questions. So keep your heart open and keep your eyes attentive to find the answers to these questions. Below I have placed the Change Cycle Chart from the change cycle website at Changecycle.com.

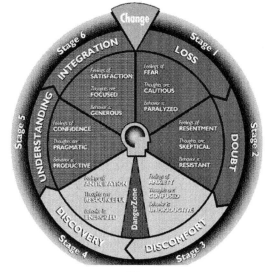

Question #1: Why do we feel like we are going to lose everything when God asks us to do something that we know we can't do on our own? This would be Stage 1 on the change cycle chart:

Stage 1: LOSS

This stage starts when we set a new goal in our lives or maybe God has asked us to do something that is way out of our comfort zone, which if it is from God, trust me, it will be way out of our comfort level. We tend to set easy goals for ourselves, goals that we know that we can reach by ourselves, but when God sets goals for us it's never easy and we feel that they are unreachable. If it is always easy then we would have no problem going through life, but when it's hard that's when we start fighting against it. I know we all have testimonies on this very thing, so in this chapter I will give you my testimony from when God called me to preach His Word and to help the hurting people who I come in contact with.

What happens in our minds when we start something new, something that is hard and very uncomfortable? We have feelings of <u>Fear</u>; thoughts of <u>Caution</u>; and our behavior is <u>Paralyzed</u>. The first thing that comes to mind is, "what will I lose by doing this?" We fear what we do not know. If it is something that we have not done before we will start to imagine the worst type of outcome. This has happened every time I started a new journey in my life. Fear, fear and more fear took over my mind, until I couldn't even take a step forward. Fear means "False Evidence Appearing Real" it is a distressing emotion that comes over us when we are faced with a new goal or a new challenge. We start imagining what could happen before it ever does. On most occasions the fear had completely taken over my mind causing me to reason my way out of my calling. Giving me thoughts of caution and caution means to have a warning against something. As the fear set in the caution took over and my behavior was to "STOP and QUIT." I was paralyzed out of fear and I couldn't take that first step. I would end up talking myself out of it because it didn't feel good and I didn't want to push through and overcome.

After I received Christ as my savior I was good with where I was, I really didn't want to change everything. I was learning His Word and how much He loved me and that was good enough for me. Until one day I heard the Lord say, "Paula I have called you to preach my gospel to hurting people around the world." I paused for a minute and said "Oh no Lord, I can't do that." In a way I was right, I couldn't do that, but He could through me. So after having the feelings of fear, the thoughts of caution and becoming paralyzed I started to talk my way out of this new journey. I had so many excuses why I couldn't do this. My legs were shaking like I had an earthquake inside of me and my heart was pounding a million beats per minute, but I knew that God had spoken to me, I just didn't know how to start.

I had a fire inside my heart that no one could put out. I was so hungry and thirsty to learn more and do what He asked me to do, but I didn't know how to get started. I got to the point to where I really didn't care what I lost, because I knew what God had in store for me was so much better than what I had for myself. So I made a decision to press through Stage 1 and step out, even in my fear. My heart was on fire to teach the Word of God and to tell my story of redemption and victory even though I was fearful. I knew that I had to step out and see what was around that next corner. So I did, I did it afraid, but I did it.

Question #2: Why do we have thoughts of doubt when we step out to start a new goal? This would be Stage 2 on the change cycle chart:

Stage 2: DOUBT

This stage starts right after we take our first step towards a new goal. Right after I heard the Lord tell me to go and preach His Word to the hurting, doubt hit me like a ton of bricks. My husband and I were attending our local Church in West Texas when I went to the Pastor and told him that I heard from the Lord and I felt in my spirit that He wanted me to preach His message to hurting people all around the world. The Pastor's response back to me was "Women aren't allowed to speak in Churches, so this couldn't have been from God." I left that day with feelings of <u>Resentment</u>;

my thoughts were Skeptical; and my behavior was Resistant. I knew in my heart that I truly heard from God and I knew that He wanted me to tell my story and to preach His Word, but I wanted to know for sure that this was really God that I was hearing. I wasn't educated enough in Church traditions so it was easy to steer me in a different direction than what I was feeling in my spirit. I was still a very young Christian and believed pretty much anything anyone told me. I didn't understand about different denominations, religions or traditions in the Churches, so I was easily steered away from God's call in my life. I started thinking, "Surly God knew I was a woman when He called me, so why would He ask me to preach His Word if in His Word it says women can't preach?" I found the scripture my Pastor gave me that confirmed what he said and sure enough there it was in 1 Corinthians 14:34-36 - *Let your women keep silence in the churches: for it not permitted unto them to speak; but they are commanded to be under obedience, as also saith the law. [35] And if they will learn anything, let them ask their husbands at home: for it is a shame for women to speak in the church.*

Can you say heartbroken? It felt like a bomb had just gone off in my heart, this brought doubt to my mind. Maybe I didn't really hear from God, or maybe I missed Him somehow. Why do I have this fire in my heart to preach the gospel, if I wasn't allowed to do so? And why would God be so mean to lead me on this path? All these thoughts were flooding my mind and my heart. I started having feelings of resentment before I even got out of the Church building. I was mad at God for telling me one thing and then not really meaning it. For months I resisted God and His calling on my life. I didn't even want to read the Word I was so mad and hurt. "Why would He set me up this way, just to fail? What kind of God could do this anyway?" I was so confused with all this, because you see I watched Joyce Meyer on T.V. every morning. Did God not know she was a woman? How she was able to preach God's Word and not me was more than I could handle. Very confused, I was feeling that maybe I wasn't good enough. This stage I think is one of the hardest stages we'll have to go through when trying to move forward on a new goal or vision in our lives. Satan's biggest tool is doubt. If he can get us to doubt the call of God on our lives, then he can defeat us in many areas. This stage will take you out of the presence of God every time, if we don't stand strong and believe.

Question #3: Why do we have discomfort and anxiety when we feel the fear and doubt coming on us? This would be Stage 3 on the change cycle chart.

Stage 3: DISCOMFORT

This is the stage that most Christians find themselves stuck in. They don't move forward and they really don't move backwards, they are just stuck. The first thing we do when we receive a word from God is put it into our minds and roll it around and around. We ponder and we think and then we ponder some more and think some more. Do you know that we can really over think God's call for us? Yes we can, until we think ourselves right out of it. It happens a lot more than you think. When we find ourselves at this place of over thinking a word from God, we enter into Stage 1 which is Loss, what will I lose if I step out and do this. Then we enter into Stage 2 which is Doubt, we receive thoughts of doubt, how can this really be God? Then we end up here at Stage 3 which is Discomfort. In this stage we will have feelings of Anxiety, our thoughts are Confused, and our behavior is Unproductive. Does this sound familiar to you?

This stage is where I was right after talking to my Pastor about what I felt God placed on my heart. Please, understand I love all Churches and I support all denominations. If they are for Jesus Christ then I am for them and we can work together to tell the gospel story of our risen Savior. Religion and tradition started way back long ago and continues today through most denominations. They really don't know why they have certain traditions like they do, but they do and continue to practice them not really even knowing why. My Pastor at that Church was an amazing man of God and I learned so much from him and I thank God for everything he taught me. But, I knew deep down inside my heart that God had called me to preach His gospel and that there had to be something that I was missing. The longer I sat and did nothing about this call, the more feelings of anxiety I had. I was confused as to what I heard, "Did I really hear from God? Am I really hearing His voice or am I just making all this up?" So with all this going on in my head I was unproductive. I did nothing. All I did was grumble in my heart and in my mind. This is the stage that defeats many, many people in reaching their goals.

On the change chart, you'll see between Stage 3 and Stage 4 it's called the Danger Zone. This is the place where we normally stop and dismiss the call or the goal. "It's too hard, I can't do it, maybe God really didn't talk to me, or maybe it's just the flesh telling me that I could not possibly reach this goal." Then we hear those six words that defeat us every time, "I CAN'T DO IT, I QUIT." If we quit here at the danger zone we will have to return back to the top and start all over again. Some people never reach their goals in life because they quit at the danger zone. I heard this not too long ago, "If you're tired of starting over, then quit giving up." How very true this statement is for many of us.

The Danger Zone:

Right here is where I had an opportunity to quit or to push through and go to Stage 4. I'm so very happy to say I chose to push through. I didn't receive the answer that my Pastor gave me on that day, I wanted to know for myself if God really called me or not. So I wrote a letter to Joyce Meyer and asked how she got past this Scripture in God's Word that says, "Women are not allowed to speak in Church?" This is where I pushed through and took that next step of faith. I really didn't feel that I would hear back from her, because she had millions of people writing letters to her every day, why would she pull my letter out and answer it or why wouldn't she? There I was with feelings of Loss, Doubt and Discomfort, then four weeks later I received a reply back. She took the time to write a letter back to me. I looked very closely at the letter to see if her name was stamped or if it was hand written and to my surprise it was hand written, to me from her personally with a Word from God. Here's the letter she wrote to me dated February 12, 2003.

Dear Paula,

Thank you for your inquiry. In answer to your questions concerning women teachers, I wish to refer you to a book written by Kenneth Hagin entitled "The Woman Question." This book expounds well on this controversial subject, and I found it to be the most thorough and efficient tool to use in answering inquires such as yours.

I realize that the Scriptures concerning women teachers and preachers have presented controversy in many churches. In taking a few lines of Scripture out of context, many people have disregarded the anointing on the lives of women as God chooses to call them and use them in the body of Christ. God's Word tells us that there is no distinction between male and female, and that the Holy Spirit calls and gives His gifts to us as He wills.

I encourage you to judge the teaching by the spiritual food that you receive and by the anointing that is on the Word to set the people free. I pray that the Holy Spirit will give the revelation, peace, and settledness that you are seeking in this area.

Thank you again for your inquiry. I send my love.
I care about you
Joyce Meyer

What would have happened if I didn't push through my fears, resentment and anxieties that awaited me at Stage 3? How many lives would have been different today if I would have stopped and quit? What would my life be like if I hadn't pushed through all these feelings and thoughts in my mind, telling me I couldn't do it? I would hate to think about the hurting people that might not have received Jesus Christ as their personal Savior if I would have stopped. So glad that I listened to my heart and reached out to find the truth.

Question #4: Why do we feel like for the first time that we have discovery and feel energized to see it through? This would be Stage 4 on the change cycle chart:

Stage 4: DISCOVERY

You better believe when I received that letter back from Joyce Meyer I was on fire. I had discovered that I was called by God, that He really did called me to preach His Word to people that were hurting all over the world. I knew now that I wasn't making this up, that I really heard from God. So I started digging into the Word of God to find out more and what my next step was. I had feelings of <u>Anticipation</u>; my thoughts were <u>Resourceful</u>; and my behavior was <u>Energized</u>. I was on fire, hungry and thirsty for all God had for me. I wanted His spirit to immerse me completely. I didn't have feelings of anxiety anymore; I was anticipating my next step with a song in my heart and joy in my spirit. I was ready for whatever direction God had for me. My thoughts and my eyes were on God and I was able to deal skillfully and promptly with the new goals that He sat before me. I got the book written by Kenneth Hagin called "The Woman Question" and I began to read and study every line. I got out the Word of God and looked up every scripture mentioned in the book. I got a Jewish Bible so that I could read the original text written by Paul when he wrote the book of Corinthians. I wanted to know the truth, so I rolled up my sleeves and I dug in with both feet.

I would like to give you an insert from the book written by Kenneth Hagin and I would like to share with you what I discovered for myself.

Remembering these things about our texts will help you understand them: (1) Paul is not talking about all women, but about wives. (2) He is talking about learning something and asking questions (1 Corinthians 14:35, 1 Timothy 2:11). Translate the Greek word gyne as wife, rather than woman, and these texts will make sense to you. In Timothy, Paul refers to Adam and Eve, a husband and a wife. He's dealing with a husband-and-wife proposition.

You see, there is really no great danger of women in general dictating to, domineering, or usurping authority over men in general. But wives have been known to subject their husbands to such indignity. And Paul is saying the wife is not to dictate to her husband, or usurp authority over him.

The women in that day had little or no education. Paul advised the wives if they would learn anything, to ask their husbands at home—thus implying the men were better informed than the women.

Alas, this is not always true now. Many women would die in hopeless ignorance of the principles of our holy faith if they depended on what crude, half-baked, pernicious, and fallacious ideas their husbands could communicate to them.

This book in line with the Word of God shed a huge light on this very confrontational subject through many denominations today. I don't understand why people don't want to take the time to research the truth. It seems they are just settling for what someone else believed long ago. I am so very thankful for the letter from Joyce Meyer. It really helped me to understand and has changed the course in which I took in my life.

My actions from that point on were energized and I was ready to take on the world. I knew that I had a challenge ahead of me, because not everyone would understand the truth that I received by studying the Word of God, but I knew what God called me to do and I would respectfully stand for His truth. In saying that, I respect the denominations and I work side by side with them every day. I may not agree with their doctrine, but if we can agree on Jesus Christ and how He died for our sins and that He shed His blood on the cross to save us from eternity in hell, then we have a place to start.

Question #5: Why do we feel so confidenct and productive after discovery is made? This would be Stage 5 on the change cycle chart:

Stage 5: UNDERSTANDING

In this stage I found total understanding. God tells us in His Word that "my people perish from a lack of understanding" that's in Hosea 4:6. In Stage 5 we will have feelings of <u>Confidence</u>; and our thoughts will be <u>Pragmatic</u>; and our actions will be <u>Productive</u>. If you'll notice this stage is completely opposite of Stage 3. In Stage 3 we had feelings of anxiety and we were confused and unproductive, here in Stage 5 that is not the case at all. If you push through and get past the danger zone and enter into Stages 4, 5 & 6, then you will find out that this goal can actually be obtained. I had found truth, so that brought confidence to my calling. I knew the truth of God's Word and that really set a fire in me that no man could put out. Revelation 3:7 states that *"What He opens, no one can close and what He closes, no one can open."* When you have found God's truth there is no man who can ever take that away from you. Not saying they won't try, because they will. This is still happening to me today, but I continue to stand on the Word of God and I push through and I am walking in God's full call for my life. Many people have made life changing decisions, because I pushed through my own feelings and accepted my call from God. I have pushed through and did what God asked me to do. Confidence is the one place satan attacks the most. If he can take your confidence away from you then he has won the battle over you. Do not let him have it, study the Word of God and find out for yourself what God has in store for you.

During this stage my thoughts were pragmatic and I was focused on the call. I set my eyes on the goal and I ran my race. In 2 Timothy 4:7 Paul writes, *"I have fought the good fight, I have finished the race, and I have kept the faith."* I remember when my husband and I went to a Ministers' conference, one of the speakers said, "When running a race you do not at any time want to come off the track and go into the stands and plead your case to others." What he was saying was, when you run a race you keep your eyes focused on the goal line. There will always be people in the grandstands yelling out to you, telling you how to run the race and 99.9% of the time they will give you their opinions and advice, but not always will it be the right advice. He told us "If you take the time to 'STOP' racing and go into the stands to argue with them you are getting out of the race." I don't want to stop running the race God has put in front of me, so I made a choice to not argue with the spectators. They have their opinion and sometimes it does not match what I have in my heart that God has told me to do, so I stay focused and I run my race. The winner of the race will be the one that stays focused on the goal that has been set before them, not the ones that stop and start, stop and start and stop and start again. This has been the best advice that I have ever received in my walk with the Lord and that is to stay focused and know in your heart that this is the race that God gave you to run.

Question #6: Why for the first time do we feel satisfied and complete? This would be Stage 6 on the change cycle chart:

Stage 6: INTEGRATION

In this stage, I found wholeness in my call. My feelings were <u>Satisfaction</u>, my thoughts were <u>Focused</u>, and my behavior was <u>Generous</u>. For the first time in my life I felt complete satisfaction. When God calls you and you don't step out towards that call, you will not feel satisfied. You will search and search for the world's ways to satisfy and complete the emptiness inside of you, but you will never find it in the world. The only way you can reach and find the satisfaction you are seeking is if you step towards the call of God and not the call of the world.

During this stage your thoughts will be focused on the goal sitting before you, and you will run the race with integrity and faith. You will find God's favor and blessings all around you. Your feelings will be very generous. You'll find ways to help others in their walk with God and you will wake up with a burning desire to help and do the will of God each and every day. That's why I'm writing this book, I want everyone to know that God has called you to do great things in your life. Sometimes it won't be easy, but you can obtain them with understanding and faith. In this chapter you will see what our minds go through as we step out in this call, so maybe after reading this book you will recognize the symptoms and push through knowing that your call from God is obtainable. Run your race, keep the faith and know that in His Presence is where you will find the strength to overcome feelings of loss, doubt and discomfort.

The Lord spoke to me as I was writing this chapter and gave me a great way to explain the change cycle, using the transformation of the butterfly. So here is the process of a butterfly.

A butterfly starts out as a caterpillar crawling on its belly everywhere it goes. They are stepped on, kicked around and viewed as something of no value. Realizing that life could be much better, they will attach themselves "head down" to a twig on a bush or tree. They make the decision to stay and go through whatever needs to happen to make this change in their life. When we start to take a step out towards the call of God in our lives we need to get somewhere alone and put our "heads down" and pray. The caterpillar starts by shedding its outer skin and it begins the transformation into a pupa (chrysalis or liquefying), a process which is completed in a matter of hours. The pupa resembles a waxy, jade vase and becomes increasingly transparent as the process progresses. We too need to become transparent or liquefied before God and before ourselves. "God, this is who I am, I hide nothing from you. Shape me and mold me into what you want me to be." I think this is one of the hardest things we have to go through, shedding our flesh and becoming transparent before God and before ourselves. The caterpillar completes the miraculous transformation into a beautiful "adult" butterfly in about two weeks. If you'll notice the part where the butterfly liquefies itself only takes a few hours, but the full transformation takes close to two weeks. Our transformation doesn't happen overnight, there is a long process we have to go through before we are transformed into what God wants us to be. This is the stage where I struggled and fought, kicking and screaming the whole way. I wanted to transform quickly, but God is not in the business of overnight breakthroughs and quick sprints. His purpose is to teach us how to run the race of a life time; He is looking for the "Marathon Racers" not sprinters. Life is not a sprint, it's a marathon. After the caterpillar goes through this very hard journey of taking off the old and putting on the new, it starts to break free from the cocoon and inflates its wings from a pool of blood that it has been stored in. When we begin to break free from our fleshly, corrupted and sinful ways, we will find out that we were covered in the Blood of Jesus. After the butterfly breaks free from the cocoon it will rest to gain its strength. After we have overcome and find that we have discovery, understanding and satisfaction we can rest in His Presence. We should at that time praise Him and thank Him for loving us so much. The butterfly then waits until its wings stiffen and dry before it flies away to start its brand new life in freedom. The butterfly is a symbol of "Freedom" and now you know the reason why.

When God asked me to explain the transformation of the butterfly, I was walking in the park. I started thinking about the similarities of the change cycle and the butterfly. I was so energized to write it down so that I wouldn't forget. I had a few miles left on my walk when the Lord immersed me in His Presence. Let me explain.

Every morning I go for a walk at my local park, this is my time with the Lord, to listen and talk with Him without interruptions. No one goes with me, I don't take my phone; it's just me and God for one hour every morning. As I walk, I talk to Him and sometimes I'll just stand in awe and Praise Him for what He is doing in my life. As I was walking the other day I was on the trail that went through the trees. You see this park has five miles of trails and paths going in and out of the trees. Such a beautiful place and the Presence of the Lord awaits me there every time. On this particular day I was talking with the Lord about this chapter in my book. I knew that I was going to write about the change cycle and what our minds go through, everything we are faced with a new goal in our lives. As I was walking I felt the Lord tell me to write about the butterfly and the transformation it has to go through to become a butterfly. I thought to myself that would really work in this chapter, so I said, "Yes let's do it God." As I walked along the path for a few minutes praying and talking to God, I came to a place just over the bridge and into the trees. I was by myself just enjoying the moment when all of a sudden I felt the Presence of the Lord so thick that I could hardly stand on my feet. As I looked around there were hundreds of butterflies all around me. I'm not talking about only a few; I'm talking about hundreds of them. They started swarming me from every direction, it felt like I was totally immersed in butterflies. I started to swat them away and then I hear the voice of the Lord say to me, "Stop and look at them." It was like God was confirming His Word to me in the physical. Butterflies were everywhere flying, flipping, playing and chasing each other as though they were so free and happy. They were in my hair, some were on my shoulders and some attached themselves to my shirt, they had no fear of me whatsoever. It was so beautiful, right there at that moment God flooded me with His Presence. He told me that the butterflies were free and that they had been born again. They had been given a brand new life. He told me that although they had to go through a very hard time to get there, they did it and now they were free. As I stood there immersed in His Presence I thought to myself, I have always heard the voice of God talking to me through my spirit, but this time He was showing what He was saying to my heart. This had to have been God, because I walk there every day and this had never happened before or since that day. God was touching me with His Words on that day through all those butterflies. As I stood there I realized that the butterflies had so much freedom and happiness. I felt the Lord say to me, "Where there is freedom there is no fear." If we are truly freed by the Blood of Jesus Christ then we should not ever fear anything that is bigger than us. These little butterflies didn't fear me in anyway; actually they wanted to show me how happy they were and how free they were. They were touching my heart and this will have an everlasting effect on my life. How encouraging that moment was for me and I pray that it is encouraging for you as well. Just know that where freedom is, fear cannot be. So as you move towards your goal stay in His Presence and be free.

Every time I find myself going through something really hard, I always find the answers I seek when I fall on my knees. I am so thankful that God loves me and that He hears every cry from my heart. What matters to you, matters to God. He will fill you up today right where you are and you will experience His Presence.

Search me, O God, and know my heart; test me and know my anxious thoughts. Point out anything in me that offends you, and lead me along the path of everlasting life.

Psalm 139:24-25

Chapter 5
The Scarlet Letter

Romans 8:1
So now there is no condemnation
for those who belong to Christ Jesus.

The scarlet letter started in the 17th century, when a woman committed sexual sin. She was led from the town <u>prison</u> with "a rag of <u>scarlet</u> cloth" on the breast of her dress that had the shape of a letter "A." This letter represents the act of sin that she had committed. Normally this sin was adultery, but a sin is a sin no matter what you do. The scarlet letter was a "symbol" of her sin or a "<u>badge of shame</u>" for all to see. We don't actually wear a big scarlet "A" on our shirts, but we do walk around in condemnation and in shame for all to see. Condemnation takes the place of the scarlet letter. "Shame" is what we really call it. You can actually trace this back to the beginning of time with Adam and Eve. The apple was the scarlet letter for Eve. Even though God told Adam not to eat of the tree in the center of the garden, Eve got the blame. Adam was her husband and he could have insisted she not eat the apple, but he didn't and ate with her. Thinking about it now, the apple could have been red and the scarlet letter was red, but then so was the blood of Jesus.

Have you ever wondered why they chose to use an "A" for the symbol of shame? There are 26 letters in the alphabet, why did they choose the letter "A?" I think I can sum that up for you in three words: "Accused, Abandoned, and Alone."

- **Accused** – to charge one with the fault, offense, or a crime; or to be blamed for wrong doing.
- **Abandoned** – to be forsaken, deserted, discarded or rejected.
- **Alone** – to be separate, apart, or isolated from others.

Can you see now why they used the letter "A?" When someone has committed sin they are first accused then abandoned and they normally end up alone. Romans 3:23-24 - *for all have sinned and fall short of the glory of God, 24 being justified freely by His grace through the redemption that is in Christ Jesus.* Even though I had received Jesus as my personal Savior I still walked around with the scarlet letter on my chest. Satan didn't have to do anything, because I did this all by myself. I was my worst enemy. I had a very hard time forgiving myself. I could forgive every one that hurt me and I could even ask for forgiveness of those I had hurt. But when it came to me forgiving me, I couldn't do it. I knew deep down inside that Jesus said He forgave me, but I really didn't feel it in my heart. I know I'm not alone here, because most people have this very same problem. We walk around today in the 21st century wearing the scarlet letter upon our chests. We walk around in shame and condemnation.

It took me five years after I had received Jesus Christ as my Savior, for me to understand that my sins were really gone. That Jesus truly forgave me and that He didn't hold my sin to use against me. In Hebrews 8:12 Jesus tells us - *For I will be merciful to their iniquities and their sins will I remember no more* , and in Hebrews 10:18 it tells us - *Now where there is absolute remission (forgiveness and cancellation of the penalty) of these [sins and law-breaking], there is no longer any offering made to atone for sin.* When Jesus went to the cross and died for our sins, it was finished. If Jesus can forgive me, why can't I forgive myself? We are sometimes our worst enemy; satan doesn't have to do anything, because we do it ourselves. When we do not receive the forgiveness that Jesus died to give to us, we become desolate. Desolate means - to be empty, forsaken, abandoned; to put guilt on or to feel condemned and shame. Tell me, does this sound like the scarlet letter to you?

In the Old Testament King David's daughter Tamar is the perfect example of this. We can find this story in 2 Samuel 13:20 - *Her brother Absalom said to her, "Has that Amnon, your brother, been with you? Be quiet now, my sister; he is your brother. Don't take this thing to heart." And Tamar lived in her brother Absalom's house, a desolate woman.* Oh my goodness, this verse gets me every time I read it. Tamar had been sexually abused by her brother Amnon and her other brother Absalom told her to be quiet and not take this to heart. "Don't take it to heart" are you kidding me? How can you not take something like this to heart? You know she felt all kinds of condemnation and shame. I can only imagine the look on her face, when her brother said, "Be quiet and don't take it to heart." I can't even imagine her feelings as she heard her brother say, "Why don't we just slap a big ol' red scarlet letter on your chest and put you in a room for the rest of your life?" She lived in her brother Absalom's house, "a desolate woman."

I feel that we continue this tradition today. We ask Jesus to forgive us, but we really never receive His full forgiveness. Most of the time we live our lives as desolate people. We allow condemnation to rule our lives and take away our joy. In John 10:10 the Bible tells us that Jesus came that we may have and enjoy life, and have it in abundance (to the full, till it overflows) but, in reality we don't. What about the woman that was caught in adultery and was taken to the temple to be stoned to death? As she knelt in the center of all those people awaiting her death, she heard the most amazing thing, "The Sound of Grace." The sound of Grace is the sound of the stones falling from the hands of her accusers. That had to have sounded so good to her at that moment. When the stones fell and hit the ground it made "The Sound of Grace." No one in that circle could cast the first stone, because they too have committed sin.

Let's read this incredible story found in John 8:1-12. *Jesus returned to the Mount of Olives, ² but early the next morning he was back again at the Temple. A crowd soon gathered, and he sat down and taught them. ³ As he was speaking, the teachers of religious law and the Pharisees brought a woman who had been caught in the act of adultery. They put her in front of the crowd. ⁴ "Teacher," they said to Jesus, "This woman was caught in the act of adultery. ⁵ The law of Moses says to stone her. What do you say?" ⁶ They were trying to trap him into saying something they could use against him, but Jesus stooped down and wrote in the dust with his finger. ⁷ They kept demanding an answer, so he stood up again and said, "All right, but let the one who has never sinned throw the first stone!" ⁸ Then he stooped down again and wrote in the dust. ⁹ When the accusers heard this, they slipped away one by one, beginning with the oldest, until only Jesus was left in the middle of the crowd with the woman. ¹⁰ Then Jesus stood up again and said to the woman, "Where are your accusers? Didn't even one of them condemn you?"* [11] *"No, Lord,"* *she said. And Jesus said, "Neither do I. Go and sin no more."* The one person that has the right to accuse her chose not to and He chooses not to accuse you either.

Jesus loves us so much that He died to take away our sins. Jesus made the choice to go all the way. He said, "It is finished." If Jesus, the perfect Son of God, can forgive us of our sins, then why can't we forgive ourselves? I finally heard God say this to me, "I love you so much that I sent my son to die for you. I forgave you for the sins that you have committed. You can't turn back time and you can't have do overs in life, that's why I sent my son to die for you. So let go of the past and go forward with Me." This Word from God changed my life forever.

I once heard this quotation and it is very powerful, so I want to share it with you. "The rearview mirror is a small glimpse into your past, but keep looking through the windshield because the view to your future is much bigger than the view to your past." How true that is in so many ways. Let go of the past and reach forward to your future with God. Forgive yourself and receive the forgiveness of Jesus Christ. It's much better on the side of forgiveness than on the side of condemnation and shame. Start today and forgive yourself, you can't turn back time and you can't have do overs, it's over and done with. Today is a new day. Take a deep breath and know that God loves you so much. Today is a gift from God and tomorrow is a bright future, receive His forgiveness and be made whole. Then and only then will you truly find yourself standing in His Presence.

Chapter 6
My Soul Longs for You

Psalm 63
O God, you are my God; I earnestly search for you.
My soul thirsts for you; my whole body
longs for you in this parched and weary land
where there is no water.

W hy stay in the mud puddles when there is an ocean on the other side of the fence? Why do we spend our time in the shallow muddy waters when we can experience the fullest of the deep blue ocean? It seems that most Christians never go deep with God; they stay in the shallow parts of God's Word, when in truth God's Word is so very deep. We choose to stay in the shallows of comfort, when the blessings are in the deep. As we embark on this incredible journey I pray that you will start to thirst and long for more of God. We will be taking a journey through the book of Psalms and see how King David longed to be in the Presence of God. I want to take you to a place that is deep and before you know it you'll find yourself wanting more. I pray that this chapter will help you find the deepest parts of God's heart. That you will cry out to Him to go deeper than you ever have before. So let's curl up in the Presence of God as our hearts walk through the book of Psalms, as we witness a powerful relationship between King David and God.

Oh, Lord, I pray that You speak through me as I write these words down on paper. I pray that Your Spirit fills our hearts, our minds and our souls. We want to know and feel what King David felt as he cried out for more of You, oh God. Let each of us experience the closeness that he felt as he searched for the depths of You, God. Let these words penetrate our hearts as we journey through the parched and weary lands where there is no water. Let our souls long for only You, oh God. Fill us now with Your un-matchless love and presence. Speak to us oh God, speak to us today and fill us now with Your Spirit. We cry out for all of You, oh God, search our hearts and change us to be more like You. Our desire is to go deeper with You God, not to stay in the place of comfort, but to go deeper in the depth of Your heart, oh God. Lead us, guide us in the deep waters of Your love. In the name of Jesus we pray.

I chose King David and the book of Psalms to explain the depths of God's love for each of us and how we can go deeper with God. If any person in the Bible knew what it was like to make mistakes daily and cry out to God to fill him and search his heart, that would be, King David. I can so relate to him in so many ways. After I received Jesus as my personal Lord and Savior, I knew that walking in His ways would not always be easy and I knew that I needed to learn how to go deeper with God and not just stay in the shallow waters. I found myself reading the book of Psalms daily and I found myself crying out to God for more. Let's take a look at the life of King David and let's tap into the secret that he had to go deeper with God and let's find out why God called King David a man after His own heart.

According to the Hebrew Bible, King David was the second King of the United Kingdom of Israel and according to the New Testament Gospels of Matthew and Luke, King David was an ancestor of Jesus. What an incredible legacy to have, right? Even though King David was a powerful King, he had many, many faults. Just like the rest of us, King David allowed his mind to override his spirit, which caused him to sin over and over again. Even through all of his mistakes, trials and sins, God still called King David a man after His own heart. 1 Samuel 13:14 *But now your kingdom must end, for the LORD has sought out a man after his own heart. The LORD has already appointed him to be the leader of his people.*

When King David was only a shepherd boy he was anointed to become the King of Israel and then eventually the ancestor of Jesus Christ, the King of Kings and the Lord of Lords, God in the flesh. I'm sure that King David had no idea what was in his future when we was out in the fields tending to his Father's sheep. You see God has big plans for all of us, but we only see what is right in front of us. Most of us would completely freak out if we knew the plans that God has for our lives. When I received Jesus as my personal Lord and Savior back in 1997, I had no idea that I would be where I am today, preaching the Gospel of Jesus Christ all over the United States leading thousands of people to Him and being a Co-Pastor to a thriving growing Church, or even writing this book. If I had known what God had planned for me back in 1997 I would have tried figuring out the how and when of His plan. God, when are you going to do this? God, how are you going to do this? Why God, When God, How God? I guess that's the reason why He doesn't tell us everything. You see before I received Jesus as my Lord and Savior, I didn't like Church or Church people. My Father was an atheist and we didn't believe in Church or Jesus. I was taught to run from these things, not become one of them. That was far, far away from any thought in my mind. God knew this, but

He had a plan for me anyway. I had to learn to walk through the journey with Him, learning more about His love for me, just like King David had to do. I had to seek out His Word and go deeper each and every second that I took a breath. I had to make a choice to go deep and get into the Presence of God to find where He wanted me to go. Just like King David I prayed that my heart be like God's. I prayed day and night to know God more, to know His full love for me. I prayed as King David prayed in Psalm 139:23-24 - *Search me, O God, and know my heart; Try me, and know my anxieties; 24 And see if there is any wicked way in me, and lead me in the way everlasting.* How many times did I pray that same prayer? You know my heart oh God, you know my anxieties oh God you know my fears, my wants and my needs oh God. You see everything that is in me, lead me in the way to everlasting with you oh God. Can you feel the fullest of God as you read this prayer? I feel the need to say that when you pray and ask God to show you the wicked things in your heart be ready, because He will. Just like King David I made many mistakes, but I always cried out to God to pick me up and help me to become more like Him.

King David always knew that he was human and that he wasn't going to be perfect. Every time King David sinned and there were many times recorded in the Bible, the first thing he did, is he fell on his knees and ask God to forgive him and to teach him to be better. I love the book of Psalms because it betrays a man that is so deeply in love with God and wants so much to be like Him. What my souls longs for, is to be deeply in love with God and to be what He created me to be.

Let's reflect back on chapter 2 of this book, we read about the Body, Soul and Spirit. The body contains our five senses; which are taste, touch, smell, sight and hearing. Our soul is our mind, feelings and emotions. Our flesh will normally always follows where the mind goes, so we can pretty much say that the flesh and soul is one unit together. The soul and the flesh will always act as one. Then, we have our spirit. Our spirit is created and filled with the Presence of God when we receive Jesus Christ as our Lord and Savior. Your spirit at that time is made perfect in every way, but your soul and your flesh are not. Just like King David I struggled with my thoughts and feelings constantly. I felt the Spirit of God inside me and I knew that He was there every second of the day, but my mind, my flesh, my emotions and my feelings were still very much in the world. This was the same battle that King David found himself in many, many times. He was warring inside himself against his soul and spirit. Let's look at Psalm 62, this was written by King David when he was in the desert running from his enemies. You will see that he was in a battle with his soul and spirit, not with people. Our soul can be our worst enemy at times. Psalm 62 - *I wait quietly before God, for my victory comes from him. ² He alone is my rock and my salvation, my fortress where I will never be shaken. ³ So many enemies against one man, all of them trying to kill me. To them, I'm just a broken-down wall or a tottering fence. ⁴ They plan to topple me from my high position. They delight in telling lies about me. They praise me to my face but curse me in their hearts. ⁵ Let all that I am wait quietly before God, for my hope is in him. ⁶ He alone is my rock and my salvation, my fortress where I will not be shaken. ⁷ My victory and honor come from God alone. He is my refuge, a rock where no enemy can reach me. ⁸ O my people, trust in him at all times. Pour out your heart to him, for God is our refuge. ⁹ Common people are as worthless as a puff of wind, and the powerful are not what they appear to be. If you weigh them on the scales, together they are lighter than a breath of air. ¹⁰ Don't make your living by extortion or put your hope in stealing. And if your wealth increases, don't make it the center of your life. ¹¹ God has spoken plainly, and I have heard it many times: Power, O God, belongs to you; ¹² unfailing love, O Lord, is yours. Surely you repay all people according to what they have done.*

In this chapter we see that King David starts out by telling God, "I will wait quietly before You, for You are my victory. You are my rock and my Salvation, I will not be shaken." Then all of a sudden his mind takes over and starts rehearsing defeat. Then in verse 5 we see that he quickly gathers his thoughts and gets them back in line with God. "Let all that I am wait quietly before You, for my hope is in You. You alone are my rock and my Salvation, I will not be shaken. My victory comes from You alone, oh, God, no enemy can reach me." Then immediately his mind takes over, rehearsing defeat again. Have you ever experienced this before? Your mind starts rehearsing defeat over and over in your head like a movie that's on replay. King David realizes what's going on and immediately falls to his knees and digs deep into his spirit and pulls out what he knows is the answer and that is to get into the Presence of God quickly. Let's read what King David recorded in verse 11. *"God I hear You, You have spoken to me, and this battle is Yours, not mine. You are my rock and my Salvation, I will not be shaken, I give it all to You, oh, God."*

Do you see yourself in this scene? Boy, I do. When reading this chapter I see that the real battle is not between him and his enemies it's between his soul and his spirit. This happens to me almost every day, one minute I know that God can, but in my mind I'm not sure that He will. When God called me to become a minister of the Gospel, my mind went absolutely berserk. "What would I have to give up? What would people think? What is going to happen to my job?" Over and over in my head these thoughts rolled and rolled out of control. I found myself saying "God if You really called me then You will see me through, I know this with all my heart, so let's do it." I felt so energized and ready for the challenge, but immediately my mind would start rehearsing defeat, before I ever got started. "What will I have to give up God and what are people going to think? Did you know that I'm a woman?" Like God didn't know. "Will I have to quit my job? What about our bills, who's going to help pay the bills God?" Then I would stop and grab my head and say "No, stop this kind of thinking. This is not having faith in God, stop it." And I would fall to my knees and draw deep within my spirit and say out loud, "This is a call from God and He is my rock, my Salvation and I will not be shaken." Just like King David did, I would go back and forth and back and forth for hours. Then finally God said, "Just step out into the deep waters and see what happens, trust Me." Just like I said at the beginning of this chapter, God doesn't want us to stay in the shallow waters, He wants us to trust Him and step out into the deep. Just like the children of Israel had to do in Joshua 3:15-16 - *Now the Jordan is at flood stage all during harvest. Yet as soon as the priests who carried the ark reached the Jordan and their feet touched the water's edge, ¹⁶ the water from upstream stopped flowing. It piled up in a heap a great distance away, at a town called Adam in the vicinity of Zarethan, while the water flowing down to the Sea of the Arabah (the Dead Sea) was completely cut off. So the people crossed over opposite Jericho. ¹⁷ The priests who carried the ark of the covenant of the LORD stood firm on dry ground in the middle of the Jordan, while all Israel passed by until the whole nation had completed the crossing on dry ground.* God told the children of Israel to cross over the Jordan, which was the only way into the Promise Land. This was harvest time and the river was overflowing. God told them just trust Me and start walking, so the priests that carried the ark took that first step into the water, and right then God parted the river. They stood firm and trusted Him and all of the people were able to walk across on dry ground.

Let me ask you a question. What has God called you to do? Is there something standing between you and God's call in your life? Maybe it's not the Jordan River, but it could be something that is just as big. If so do like the Israelites did, take that first step into the unknown and trust God. He will never let you down. He said, "I will never leave you nor forsake you, not even till the end of time." Peter tells us in Acts 10:34, *"In truth I perceive that God shows no partiality."* If God did it for the Israelites, then He has to do it for you too. All He asks is that you trust Him. As the story goes with the Israelites, they crossed through the Jordan River and were on their way to the Promise Land.

Now let's look back at what happens next with King David. In the story above, King David is running from his son Absalom and his army that was trying to kill him. King David ran away to Edom. Edom is just east of Jerusalem where King David lived. To get to Edom, King David had to go through the wilderness. There was not much water and it was very dry. This is where King David was crying out because he was thirsty, not for water but he was thirsty for God's Presence. He could not go to the Temple in Jerusalem and speak to God like he normally did, so he had to fall to his knees right there in this dry and weary land and trust that God would hear his cry and yes God heard him in a big way.

Let's look at Psalm 3. This is a psalm from King David as he praised God while in the wilderness running from his son Absalom and his army. *LORD, how they have increased who trouble me! Many are they who rise up against me. ² Many are they who say of me, "There is no help for him in God." ³ But You, O LORD, are a shield for me, my glory and the One who lifts up my head. ⁴ I cried to the LORD with my voice, And He heard me from His holy hill. ⁵ I lay down and slept; I awoke, for the LORD sustained me. ⁶ I will not be afraid of ten thousands of people who have set themselves against me all around. ⁷ Arise, O LORD; Save me, O my God! For You have struck all my enemies on the cheekbone; You have broken the teeth of the ungodly. ⁸ Salvation belongs to the LORD. Your blessing is upon Your people.* After, I searched deeply into God's Word, I found the only way to win this kind of battle is to fall to your knees and cry out to God to fill you with His Presence, just like King David did. We have to start out by speaking God's Word out loud and confessing His goodness. We need to take charge over our minds, our emotions and our feelings and bring them under the submission of the Blood of Jesus Christ. Where ever you are right now, ask God what His call is for you and take that step out into the deep. Trust Him and I promise He'll never let you down.

The City of Regret,
written by Larry Harp

I had not really planned on taking a trip this time of year, and yet I found myself packing rather hurriedly. This trip was going to be unpleasant and I knew in advance that no real good would come of it. I'm talking about my annual "Guilt Trip to the City of Regret."

I got tickets to fly there on Wish I Had Airlines. It was an extremely short flight. I tried to check in my baggage, but there was no room, so I chose to carry it myself all the way. My baggage was weighted down with a thousand memories of what might have been. No one greeted me as I entered the terminal to the Regret City International Airport. I say international because people from all over the world come to this dismal town.

As I checked into the Heartbreak Hotel, I noticed that they were hosting this year's most important event, the Annual Pity Party, which was right next to the pool of misery. I wasn't going to miss that great social occasion. Many of the towns leading citizens would be there.

First, there would be the Done family, you know, Should Have Done, Would Have Done and Could Have Done. Then came the I Had family. You probably know ol' Wish I Had and his clan. The biggest family there would be the Yesterday's. There are far too many of them to count, but each one would have a very sad story to share.

Then Shattered Dreams would surely make an appearance. And It's Their Fault would regale us with stories (excuses) about how things had failed in his life, and each story would be loudly applauded by Don't Blame Me and I Couldn't Help It family.

Well, to make a long story short, I went to this depressing party knowing that there would be no real benefit in doing so. And, as usual, I became very depressed. But as I thought about all of the stories of failures brought back from the past, it occurred to me that this trip and the "pity party and the pool of misery" could be cancelled by ME! I started to truly realize that I did not have to be there. I didn't have to be depressed. One thing kept going through my mind, I can't change yesterday, but I do have the power to make the choice about today. I can be happy, joyous, fulfilled, encouraged, as well as encouraging. Knowing this, I left the City of Regret immediately and left no forwarding address. Am I sorry for mistakes I've made in the past? YES! But there is no physical way to undo them.

So, if you're planning a trip back to the City of Regret, please cancel all your reservations right now. Instead, take a trip to a place called, Starting Again. I liked it so much that I have now taken up permanent residence there. My neighbors, the I Forgive Myselfs and the New Starts are so very helpful. By the way, you don't have to carry around heavy baggage here, because the load is lifted from your shoulders upon arrival. God bless you in finding this great town. If you can find it -- it's in your own heart -- please look me up. I live on I Can Do It Street.

This is a place that King David found himself many times, the city of regret. Actually, I believe that we all have taken a trip once or twice to the city of regret and into the famous pity party. Let's take a glance back in time to when King David had an affair with Bathsheba. In this story, we'll discover that King David ordered Bathsheba to come to him and because he was the King, she had no choice. She had to follow his orders or die. Bathsheba was married to Uriah an officer in King David's army. After Bathsheba came to King David he took advantage of her and slept with her. She had just completed the purification rites after having her menstrual period when King David ordered her to come to him and because of his sinful actions, Bathsheba became pregnant. King David knew that during a woman's menstrual cycle they were considered unclean and they were not allowed to have intercourse until they completed the purification rites ordered by law. King David knew that she had not been with her husband Uriah since her purification. Because of her becoming pregnant, King David knew that he would be accused of this sin. This could really cause him lots of trouble in his kingship. So King David tricked Uriah by getting him drunk for several days and telling him that he had been with his wife during this time. When that didn't work King David sent Uriah out to the front lines of the war so that he would be killed. King David was committing murder without even being there. He was committing a sin to cover up another sin. Does this sound like something you have done? Committing a sin to cover up another sin? I have, many times and what a snowball effect it has when we do this.

Trying to cover up your sin will do nothing but take you to the city of regret. You will become depressed, angry and without repentance, you can't be set free from your sin. Let's take a look at how King David felt when Nathan the prophet came to him and told him God was angry with him about what he had done and that he needed to repent and be forgiven of his sins. In this Psalm you will see that King David was headed straight to the city of regret and was right in the middle of entering into the pity party, but quickly he realized where he was headed and fell on his knees and repented to God. This Psalm was written by King David during his darkest hour.

Psalms 32

Oh, what joy for those whose disobedience is forgiven, whose sin is put out of sight! ² Yes, what joy for those whose record the LORD has cleared of guilt, whose lives are lived in complete honesty! ³ When I refused to confess

my sin, my body wasted away, and I groaned all day long.
*⁴ Day and night your hand of discipline was heavy on
me. My strength evaporated like water in the summer
heat. ⁵ Finally, I confessed all my sins to you and stopped
trying to hide my guilt. I said to myself, "I will confess
my rebellion to the LORD." And you forgave me! All my
guilt is gone. ⁶ Therefore, let all the godly pray to you
while there is still time, that they may not drown in the
floodwaters of judgment. ⁷ For you are my hiding place;
you protect me from trouble. You surround me with songs
of victory. ⁸ The LORD says, "I will guide you along the
best pathway for your life. I will advise you and watch
over you. ⁹ Do not be like a senseless horse or mule that
needs a bit and bridle to keep it under control." ¹⁰ Many
sorrows come to the wicked, but unfailing love surrounds
those who trust the LORD. ¹¹ So rejoice in the LORD
and be glad, all you who obey him! Shout for joy, all you
whose hearts are pure!*

Can you hear the cry of David's heart as he confesses
his sins to God? He said in verse 4 that the hand of
discipline was heavy on him. Anytime we sin and
choose not to repent and make a choice to cover one sin
with another, you will enter into the city of regret and
depression. This will cause you to feel this heaviness in
your heart. You will become heavy with gilt and pain,
crying out day and night. God see's all and knows all.
You can't hide anything from Him or yourself. So if
you're at a place in your life that you are taking way
too many trips to the city of regret, then here's your

chance to repent. Ask God to forgive you and you can start planning a trip to the place of "Starting Again."

In Psalm 51 David writes in verses 7-15 - *Purify me from my sins, and I will be clean; wash me, and I will be whiter than snow. ⁸ Oh, give me back my joy again; you have broken me now, let me rejoice. ⁹ Don't keep looking at my sins. Remove the stain of my guilt. ¹⁰ Create in me a clean heart, O God. Renew a loyal spirit within me. ¹¹ Do not banish me from your presence, and don't take your Holy Spirit from me. ¹² Restore to me the joy of your salvation, and make me willing to obey you. ¹³ Then I will teach your ways to rebels, and they will return to you. ¹⁴ Forgive me for shedding blood, O God who saves; then I will joyfully sing of your forgiveness. ¹⁵ Unseal my lips, O Lord, that my mouth may praise you.*

David repented and entered into the place of praise and starting again. God tells us that He remembers our sins no more in Hebrews 8:12. This was very hard for me to understand after I received Salvation through the Blood of Jesus. I knew I was forgiven, but I had a really hard time letting go of the past. I would take that trip to the city of regret more than I would like to admit. I found myself talking about the past and becoming depressed and heavy in my heart over and over again. Jesus didn't die so that I could stay in the place of shame and bondage. He came and died so that I could be set free. I finally understood that when I repented of my sins they were gone for good. Jesus never brings our sins back up, we do.

So come on and let's board the flight to the city of "Starting Again" and find rest for your soul. You do not have to carry your heavy baggage anymore. Jesus has taken them for you. Just like King David, make that choice today - you are the only one that can. Choose today to confess your sins to God and then let them go. Enter into the land of forgiveness and let the past go, it will do nothing but weigh you down.

Although King David made many mistakes, God did call him a man after His own heart. God doesn't see the outward side of a person, He only see's the heart. God knows that people cannot be perfect, there's only one perfect person and that is Jesus Christ. King David loved God with all his heart. King David was quick to repent when he had done something wrong. He knew that the heaviness of sin would weigh him down and take him away from the Presence of God. I love it when King David wrote Psalm 139. He was talking to God and thanking Him for knowing him so deeply. Please understand God is for you, not against you. He knows your every thought before you think it and loves you anyway. He knows the mistakes that you will make and loves you anyway. We have to come to a place to where we know and trust God from the depths of our hearts. Paul talked about this in Romans 7:21-25 - *I have discovered this principle of life—that when I want to do what is right, I inevitably do what is wrong. *22* I love God's law with all my heart. *23* But there is another power within me that is at war with my mind. This power* *makes me a slave to the sin that is still within me. ²⁴ Oh, what a miserable person I am! Who will free me from this life that is dominated by sin and death? ²⁵ Thank God! The answer is in Jesus Christ our Lord.*

You have to know that Jesus Christ is the only way to freedom from sin. God knows that you are not perfect. He doesn't expect you to be. All God is asking for, is for you to love and trust Him with your whole heart. You are going to make mistakes; there is no way around it. It's going to happen. You can choose to take a trip to the City of Regret or you can choose to ask God to forgive you and move on to the city of Starting Again. For me the city of Starting Again is a much better and brighter place.

I would like to end this chapter with Psalm 139, anytime you find yourself taking that regretful trip down the past I ask you to please read this Psalm and find deep in your heart that God really loves you and knows you all so well. Psalm 139:1-18 - *O LORD, you have examined my heart and know everything about me. ² You know when I sit down or stand up. You know my thoughts even when I'm far away. ³ You see me when I travel and when I rest at home. You know everything I do. ⁴ You know what I am going to say even before I say it, LORD. ⁵ You go before me and follow me. You place your hand of blessing on my head. ⁶ Such knowledge is too wonderful for me, too great for me to understand! ⁷ I can never escape from your Spirit! I can never get away from your presence!* *8 If I go up to heaven, you are there; if I go down to the grave, you are there.* *9 If I ride the wings of the morning, if I dwell by the farthest oceans,* *10 even there your hand will guide me and your strength will support me.* *11 I could ask the darkness to hide me and the light around me to become night* *12 but even in darkness I cannot hide from you. To you the night shines as bright as day. Darkness and light are the same to you.* *13 You made all the delicate, inner parts of my body and knit me together in my mother's womb.* *14 Thank you for making me so wonderfully complex! Your workmanship is marvelous—how well I know it.* *15 You watched me as I was being formed in utter seclusion, as I was woven together in the dark of the womb.* *16 You saw me before I was born. Every day of my life was recorded in your book. Every moment was laid out before a single day had passed.* *17 How precious are your thoughts about me, O God. They cannot be numbered!* *18 I can't even count them; they outnumber the grains of sand! And when I wake up, you are still with me!*

When you know in your heart that God loves you so much and that He will never leave nor forsake you, you will experience the fullest of His Presence.

I wait quietly before God, for my victory comes from him. He alone is my rock and my salvation, my fortress where I will never be shaken.

Psalm 62:1-2

Chapter 7
Enjoying the Journey

John 10:10
The thief comes only in order to steal and kill and destroy. I came that they may have and enjoy life, and have it in abundance (to the full, till it overflows).

L ife is a journey – Not a destination! Life here on earth is only temporary. It is not our final destination. Those who want to enjoy their life must first learn how to enjoy the journey. Therefore, to have never enjoyed the journey is to have never enjoyed your life. Why would you want to go through life and not enjoy all the blessings that God has for you? Many people live life worried, stressed and unhappy. Jesus said, "I came so that you may have and enjoy life, and have it in abundance to the full, till it overflows." He didn't say, "I came so that you need to struggle day by day just to make it through till you go to heaven," but this is how many of us live our lives, struggling day by day just trying to survive, until Jesus takes us home to glory. Satan comes to steal your joy, to kill your dreams and destroy your testimony. The sad thing is, is that we let him do it. We have the power to change our lives and start walking in the fullness and joy that Jesus died to give us. We have the power to make that choice, to stop struggling and worrying about every little thing. I have seen so many people defeated because they speak defeat out of their mouths. Maybe you've heard it as well. Something like this, "Yes, I'm a Christian and I believe that Jesus died for me, 'BUT' life is just so hard. I struggle everyday just trying to make it through. I'll never be happy."

I have heard many people say, "I'll be happy when." "When I get married" then they will say, "God if you'll just take my spouse away then maybe I could be happy." Or they say, "I'll be happy when I have children," then you'll hear them say, "God these kids are driving me crazy and I'll never be happy again." Or maybe you'll hear someone say "I'll be happy when I get a bigger house," then they will say, "God I can't clean this house by myself it's much too big, I'm so unhappy." Funny isn't it? But it is so very true. I have caught myself saying these very things. I prayed for God to bless me with something I thought I wanted. When He did I still wasn't happy. That's because it's not the stuff or the people in our lives that is going to make us happy. It's the joy that only comes from Jesus being present in our lives that truly makes us happy.

Joy is a choice that we have to make each and every day. Pray this before you start your day, "I make the choice to be happy today no matter what is in store for me. I choose to not stress about every little thing. I choose to enjoy today as if it was my last day on earth. I choose to love the people around me, no matter how they act. I know that the people in my life are not going to be perfect and I know that I live on an earth that is not perfect, but that will not steal my joy today. Joy is a choice and I choose to not let satan take that away from me. I choose to enjoy my journey and I make the choice to enjoy my day no matter what." If you'll take the time to say this each and every day I promise this will make your day much brighter. Now, I'm not saying that you'll never have a bad day if you say this confession, because we do live on earth. What I am saying is that we can make a choice and say it out of our mouths that happiness is just because Jesus lives in me and for that alone I need nothing else to be happy.

Remember not to be so super spiritual that you are no good to anyone. Our actions can be a sermon spoke loud to everyone around us. Enjoy the day, but don't be so out in space that no one can reach you. There is a big difference in being spiritual and truly happy. We can put on our best face for others to think we have it all together, but people can see right through that most of the time. Being happy comes from inside not the outside. Enjoying the journey is for you to have the inner peace and love of Jesus Christ in your heart. It's you being ok with you and with who you are. That in itself speaks volumes to people and to God. 1 Peter 5:8 - *Be well balanced (temperate, sober of mind), be vigilant and cautious at all times; for that enemy of yours, the devil, roams around like a lion roaring, seeking someone to seize upon and devour.* This scripture is so very important so please hear what it is saying. Be well balanced, if you're not, the devil will devour you. Like a teeter totter, if it's not balanced on both sides it will not work the way it was designed to work. The same goes for your life. If you are unbalanced on one side you'll not enjoy your life journey. Stay balanced in God's Word and enjoy your life all together. You don't have to be a super Christian to be happy. You just need to enjoy what Jesus died to give you and that is freedom to enjoy your life. He died to give us freedom from worry, freedom from stress, freedom from strife, freedom from being confused and freedom from any type of bondage that satan has put in your path. Freedom is a very good thing and Jesus died to give us the freedom that we need to live happy lives.

This is something that I had to learn in my walk with the Lord. After I received Jesus as my personal Lord and Savior I was still in a lot of bondage, I wasn't a happy person at all. I was a person that complained and found fault with everything. I was a very negative person. I was taught to never believe in anything good, because if it didn't happen, then I would never be let down. I'm sure you are not like this, but let me explain what happened with me. My spirit was born again, but my soul and my flesh were still very much a part of the world and the ways of the world. You can't truly be happy when you have a war going on inside of you. My spirit was filled with the Spirit of God and I knew that something changed, but I still did the things I once did before I was saved. Now, in saying this, because of my Salvation I was able to kick my drug and alcohol addiction with the help of Jesus. What I am saying is that my attitude was still very negative and my actions were still in the world. My attitude was, "Well if I just don't believe in something good happening in my life, then I will not be let down when it doesn't." Sounds pretty negative huh? That was my way of thinking 99.9 percent of the time. I could find fault with everything. God had to teach me about enjoying my life. I needed His help in the process. With God, it takes two to make a change. God can make changes in your life only if you work with Him. I had to be willing to learn how much God loved me and how much He really wanted me to enjoy my journey here on this earth. I heard in my heart God tell me one morning. "Why should you stay miserable all your life when I came to the earth and died to give you a good life for you to enjoy? It is your choice to change, but I want you to know that I am here to help you and I will never leave you."

I had no confidence in who I was in Christ Jesus. It wasn't the people or the circumstances around me making me unhappy; it was me making me unhappy. It wasn't someone else's place to keep me happy; it was my place to make sure I knew who I was through the Blood of Jesus. In Ephesians 2:10 it tells us - *For we are God's [own] handiwork (His **workmanship**), recreated in Christ Jesus, [born anew] that we may do those good works which God predestined (planned beforehand) for us [taking paths which He prepared ahead of time], that we should walk in them [**living the good life** which He prearranged and made ready for us to live].* In the New Living Translation it tells us that we are God's masterpiece. Masterpiece means - a person's greatest piece of work. You are not a copy, you are God's masterpiece. The difference between a copy and a masterpiece is the masterpiece has had the hands of the Master all over it as He created His creation. That's you and me, masterpieces created by God Himself. God created you to live the good life that He prearranged and made ready for us to live and if we are not enjoying our life then we are not doing what we were created to do. Knowing this changed my life forever.

The hardest task for me to do was to forgive myself for all the bad things that I had done. I thought by condemning myself to a life of unhappiness would be a way to justify my actions for my past. But that's not what God had planned for me when He came to this earth as a baby and died on a cross for my Salvation and may I add, for my happiness. Think about this for a minute; let's look at the life of a 100 dollar bill. It was created to purchase 100 dollars' worth of stuff. After it comes from the press, it is brand new and crisp with no tears or wrinkles. Then it travels thousands of miles being handled by millions of people. It ends up being folded, wadded, washed, stepped on, trashed and sometimes torn. The value of the 100 dollar bill is still $100 anyway you look at it. It is still worth $100. Just because it has gone through a lot in its lifetime, it's still very valuable to the person that owns it. Do you not think God loves you more than a 100 dollar bill? You are valuable to God and He has forgiven you of all your sins. Psalm 103:12 states, *He has removed our sins as far from us as the east is from the west.* Hebrews 8:12 states, *and I will forgive their wickedness, and I will never again remember their sins.* These two scriptures were so freeing to me. If God doesn't hold my sins against me then why can't I forgive myself? Five years I held unforgiveness and misery in my heart for myself until I finally let it go. Unhappy people are not unhappy because of their circumstances, that's just an excuse. They are really unhappy because they have not truly received the forgiveness of Jesus Christ and they have never understood the true value of their own lives.

After I understood how much God really loved me and how valuable I was to Him, I started enjoying my journey here on this earth. It's not anyone's responsibility to keep me happy; it's my responsibility to know my value in Christ Jesus. God wants us to enjoy every day like it was our last day. We waste so much time being unhappy when happiness is right in front of you.

The 4 keys to enjoying the journey:

1. Receive the forgiveness of Jesus Christ and let Him take away your sins.
2. Forgive yourself. You can't turn back time and you can't have do overs, so let the past go and start living and enjoying your life today.
3. Learn who you are in Christ. Read God's Word about who you are to Him. Know your value in God's Kingdom. If He didn't think you were valuable then, He would have never left the Throne of Heaven to come to this earth as a baby, and then turn around and died for you. You are so very valuable to God. The quicker you understand this, the quicker you will start to enjoy your life.
4. Start speaking positive uplifting things from your mouth. No one wants to be around someone that is negative all the time. Be positive and enjoy your life. Remember no one is going to be perfect. Everyone

will fail at some point in time. Understanding this will set you free to enjoy the people around you. Failing does not make you a failure it's just a lesson learned.

In doing these four simple steps, you will find yourself in the Presence of God enjoying your life.

Chapter 8
Sold Out

Matthew 13:44
"The Kingdom of Heaven is like a treasure
that a man discovered hidden in a field. In his
excitement, he hid it again and sold everything he
owned to get enough money to buy the field.

In this parable Jesus is talking about finding a Hidden Treasure in the middle of a field and when you find it, you go and sell everything so that you can buy that field. Jesus is not talking about selling everything you have for money; He is talking about doing whatever it takes to keep that Treasure that you found. In this parable

Jesus is the Treasure that we seek. When we find Him we need to do whatever we can to keep Him in our lives. There are too many believers today that are just getting by with as little as they can. Very few believers are 100 percent sold out to Jesus. Very sad when you think about it, but it's true. Many people receive Salvation only to insure that when they die they will go to heaven. They really don't care about their journey here on earth. They want to do just enough to get them by and that's all. I don't know about you, but I want more than just enough, I want to be sold out to Jesus. That Hidden Treasure is worth more than life to me.

In Mark 4, Jesus talks about the parable of the sower and no, He is not talking about sowing money. He is talking about four different types of ground that represents the believer. When I say ground, I'm not talking about actual dirt and rocks. I am talking about Christians, people that call themselves believers of God's Word. Let's read one of the most powerful parables Jesus told in scripture. He said "if you can understand this parable then you'll understand all the parables." Jesus said, "Anyone with ears to hear should listen and understand." So I hope that I can help you to understand this parable in a way that will open up your heart to receive all that Jesus has for you. Let's take a look.

Mark 4:1-9 - *Once again Jesus began teaching by the lakeshore. A very large crowd soon gathered around him, so he got into a boat. Then he sat in the boat while all the people remained on the shore. ² He taught them by telling many stories in the form of parables, such as this one: ³ "Listen! A farmer went out to plant some seed. ⁴ As he scattered it across his field, some of the seed fell on a footpath, and the birds came and ate it. ⁵ Other seed fell on shallow soil with underlying rock. The seed sprouted quickly because the soil was shallow. ⁶ But the plant soon wilted under the hot sun, and since it didn't have deep roots, it died. ⁷ Other seed fell among thorns that grew up and choked out the tender plants so they produced no grain. ⁸ Still other seeds fell on fertile soil, and they sprouted, grew, and produced a crop that was thirty, sixty, and even a hundred times as much as had been planted!" ⁹ Then he said, "Anyone with ears to hear should listen and understand."*

The four types of ground that Jesus is talking about are:

The Footpath or The Hard Ground – This type of ground represents the people that come to Church and they hear the Word of God which is the seed and immediately the enemy comes and takes the Word away. They are defeated before they ever get started because there was no soil in their heart for the seed to be planted. I see people like this every Sunday. They come to Church only because it's something they feel they need to do. As they sit in Church and The Word is being taught, they do not hear it, because the enemy will place distractions in front of them so that he can steal the Word immediately. They will find themselves texting, looking at Facebook, or day dreaming not hearing the Word at all. Their ground is hard and the seed cannot take root. Therefore, the enemy comes immediately to take the Word away.

The Stony Ground – This type of ground represents the people that come to Church and they really desire to know more about the Word of God. So they are ready and on fire to receive. They come in overly excited and can't wait to hear the Word of God and to sing all of the songs. They will be the first ones with their hands in the air, singing the loudest and amen-ing to everything the Pastor says. But, as soon as they walk out the doors of the Church, they can't do what the Word tells them to do. The stony ground is a place where the soil is sitting on top of a rock. The seed is planted in the hearts of these people, but the roots of the seed cannot take hold, because it is planted in shallow soil. This person will receive the Word of God quickly but doesn't allow the seed to go very deep and since the seed was not planted deep; its roots cannot grab hold when the wind blows or the sun shines. Therefore the plant withers and blows away. There is no depth to their hearts and it was only for a moment that they kept the seed before the enemy came to take it away.

The Thorny Ground – This type of ground represents the people that really want to learn God's Word and has great intentions to do better and to change their lives. They come expecting the Word of God to change their life. They sincerely want to do what the Word of God tells them to do, but as soon as they get back out into the world they are choked out by the non-believers. They can't stand strong and they are choked out by the world's ways. Jesus talks about this very thing in another parable about the wheat and the weeds. The wheat is representing the Christians and the weeds are representing the non-Christians. Let's take a look at this parable in Matthew 13:24-30 - [24] *"The Kingdom of Heaven is like a farmer who planted good seed in his field.* [25] *But that night as the workers slept, his enemy came and planted weeds among the wheat, then slipped away.* [26] *When the crop began to grow and produce grain, the weeds also grew.* [27] *"The farmer's workers went to him and said, 'Sir, the field where you planted that good seed is full of weeds! Where did they come from?'* [28] *'An enemy has done this!' the farmer exclaimed. 'Should we pull out the weeds?' they asked.* [29] *'No, he replied, 'you'll uproot the wheat if you do.* [30] *Let both grow together until the harvest. Then I will tell the harvesters to sort out the weeds, tie them into bundles, and burn them, and to put the wheat in the barn."* Jesus said that He would not take believers away from the non-believers which are the weeds in this parable. He did say that He would let both coincide together and at the time of harvest if the believers stood in their faith and stood strong on the Word of God and if they don't let the world's ways take them back in, then they will receive the harvest. The reason for leaving both together would be in hopes that the believer would influence the non-believer in

97

the right way, but sometimes the believer is not strong enough and is choked out by sin and quickly falls away from the Word of God. This is where the believers need to stand strong and stay in the Word of God which gives the strength they need to make it through the world without being tempted.

The Fertile Ground – This type of ground represents the people that open up their hearts to receive the Word of God and after receiving the Word seed, they water it and tend to it every day until they receive a harvest. These are the people that are sold out to Jesus. They do whatever is needed to grow in their faith. Good ground people are not 30 percent Christians nor are they 60 percent Christians, but 100 percent sold out to Jesus Christians. Now I'm not saying that we need to be a "Super Doer Holier than Thou Christian," I'm talking about being who God made you to be, but totally sold out in love with Him. In other words, when you find the Treasure of Jesus Christ you will sell out to make sure you keep it, that's being a 100 percent Christian.

When I received Jesus in 1997, I fell totally in love with Him, wanting more and more every day. I knew that Jesus died for me and I loved Him so much for what He did. But at first I was not a 100 percent sold out Christian, I was only 30 percent devoted to Christ. I only wanted to give Him 30 percent of me, not all of me. I loved Him with everything I had, but I still didn't want to go all the way. There were still some areas in my life that I didn't feel Jesus needed to be involved in. You know those areas of your life that you would like to just hang on to a little longer. Do you have a few areas like that? It's ok because most of us do. As time went on and I learned more about Him and His love for me, I would find myself giving Him more and more of me and soon I became 60 percent sold out. Thinking that I was doing good to reach 60 percent, I was ok with that, but I still had 40 percent I wasn't dealing with. This 40 percent was my mouth and my control. I still wanted to be in control of everything and I wanted to tell others what I thought whether they wanted my input or not. Until, one day when I felt the Lord speak to me about how He gave 100 percent of Himself for me, so why couldn't I give Him 100 percent of myself? After thinking about it, it hit me like a ton of bricks. Jesus is not a 30 percent Jesus, He didn't go to the beating post and then just say, "Nope, I'm not doing this; these people are not worth it." Jesus is not a 60 percent Jesus. He didn't take the beating and then walk up Calvary's Road to the cross that awaited His death and just say, "Nope, I'm not doing this." He didn't say, "I'm not dying for their sins. I really didn't want to go that far and I think I'll just pass on the death part." My Jesus is a 100 percent Jesus. He went all the way just for you and me. He took the beating for our iniquities and our healing and He went to that old rugged cross and there He died for our sins. So for Him to ask us to become 100 percent sold out to Him you can't say no. But if you're one who doesn't want to give Him your all, then you really don't understand His Love for you.

The Jesus that I know and love so much, has an intensity of love for all humanity that is unmatched by anyone. John 3:16 says, *For God so loved the world that he gave his only Son, so that everyone who believes in Him may not perish but may have eternal life.* Today, we talk about the love of Jesus, but very few really understand the depth of that love. Being 100 percent sold out and living the abundant life for Jesus is impossible without first understanding how much He really loves us, and second, Jesus loves everyone no matter what we have done. The Jesus that I know in my heart wants you to know that He loves you more than life itself. He proved that when He went all the way to the cross and died for us.

In the life of Jesus Christ, we see a living example of the fruit of the Spirit. Jesus modeled love for us, but He did so in a way, that challenges our understanding of love. Jesus shows that love is more than just a romance or a feeling. Love is actually an action. Actions towards God and towards others. He has given us only two commandments to live by. The first is to love God above all else and the second is to love our neighbors as we love ourselves. Understanding the love of Jesus will help you become 100 percent sold out to Him. When you find the Treasure of being in His Presence then you will sell everything you have to keep it. I am a living example of this. I have asked God for many things in my life. Some were really big things and He wants to bless me with these things, but first He needs to know where I am with Him. Am I only 30 percent devoted to Him or am I 60 percent devoted or maybe I am totally sold out at 100 percent? He wants to bless me but first I have to be in His Word and I have to learn to stand in faith to receive His promises.

Jesus wants more than anything to dance with us, but first we have to get up and come out on the dance floor and grab hold of Him and dance. He can't dance alone, it take two to tango. Are you ready to dance with Jesus? Are you ready to give your all to Him, because He gave His all for you? What type of ground are you? Are you the Hard Ground, where the Word of God can't even take root, because your heart is hard and will not let Him in? What about the Stony Ground, where the Word of God takes root only for a very short time and as soon as the storms of life come at you, you can't hold on to God's Word because the root never went very deep. What about the Thorny Ground? Are you the one that receives the Word of God and plants in your heart? You are standing and trusting God for big things in your life, but as soon as you get around non-believers you fall back into sin again. Or are you the Good Fertile Ground? This is when the seed of God is planted in your heart and when it sprouts up, it produces a crop of a hundred times as much as had been planted. Think about it, what type of ground are you? The time that you put in towards learning the Word of God is what you will get out of it. Yes, you most likely will start out at each one of these grounds, but if you don't give up, you'll eventually become the good fertile ground that produces a 100 percent harvest.

I have been walking with God for a while now and I can truly say that each and every day is a gift from Him. I have made a choice to become the good fertile ground that produces good fruit and I have made a choice to give everything I have for the Treasure I have found in Jesus Christ. Remember the parable at the beginning in Matthew 13:44 - *"The Kingdom of Heaven is like a treasure that a man discovered hidden in a field. In his excitement, he hid it again and sold everything he owned to get enough money to buy the field."* Are you willing to sell out? Are you willing to do what it takes to keep the Treasure of Jesus Christ? These are questions that only you can answer. I pray that this book has touched your heart in ways that will bring you into His Presence. There is no other place that I'd rather be than in the Presence of God. That is the place of unconditional love.

Let me ask you a question, have you made Jesus Christ the Lord of your life? Have you actually said Jesus forgive me of my sins and come into my heart? This is the first step to freedom and finding that perfect Treasure. In Romans 10:9 it tells us that, *If you confess with your mouth that Jesus is Lord and believe in your heart that*

God raised him from the dead, you will be saved. There is no sin so horrible, so cruel, or unthinkable and no person so wicked that God cannot forgive and cleanse them. The Bible teaches us that God is greater than any sin. Your past behaviors, no matter how bad, cannot and will not prevent you from having a relationship with God through the Blood of Jesus. Even before you were born, God made an unchanging decision to forgive you and to love you, even knowing your sin beforehand. When Jesus died on the cross, He paid our debt in full for all of our sins. The word "Grace" can be defined as favor, or compassion. It is to get what you do not deserve. Your sin deserves judgment and punishment. Nevertheless, because you choose to confess and ask for forgiveness, you will receive Grace instead of punishment. Each time you sin, grace and forgiveness are available for you. Now, I'm not saying for you to continue in sin and just ask for forgiveness and live your life at 30 percent, what I am saying is that God gives us the ability to walk away from sin and start living the life He intended for us to have.

If you are reading this book right now and feel in your heart that you are ready to receive Jesus, I would like to lead you in this simple prayer. You need to pray this prayer from the bottom of your heart. Please bow your head and pray with me. Let's pray together. *Dear Lord, I confess to you that I am a sinner in need of a Savior. I believe that you are the son of God and I ask you to forgive me of my sins and fill this void inside me. I give my life to you today, mold me and lead me in your way. In Jesus name, Amen.* If you just prayed this prayer with me and meant it with your heart, then your name has been written in the Lamb's Book of Life. So, on that judgment day, you can stand before God and know without a doubt that you have an eternal life in Heaven. Let me add this by saying, you need to make Jesus the Lord over your life. You need to be 100 percent sold out to Him. Remember, Jesus didn't go only 30 or 60 percent of the way. He went 100 percent of the way and died for you and me. He loves you so much and all He's asking is that you come and give yourself to Him. You need to get into a Bible teaching church and learn about the Word of God and remember the four different types of ground that Jesus talks about in the parable in Mark 4. Stay alert and study His word often, because your enemy satan is out to steal the Word from your heart. Work your way through until you become the good ground. Make sure you don't give up and please be patient, you didn't get into your mess overnight and you won't get out of it overnight either. For God gives us new Grace for every day. So use the Grace for today and tomorrow's Grace will come tomorrow. You too will start to enjoy your new life through Christ Jesus, and you'll begin to see the 100 percent harvest in your life. Work hard, study His Word daily and know He loves you. To experience His Presence it takes you meeting with Jesus, taking His hand and trusting His every move. I pray that you enjoyed this book as much as I enjoyed writing it. May God truly bless you and your walk with Him. When you Experience His Presence you will never be empty again.

I will rejoice in
the Lord always.

Philippiams 4:4